eteam

The Case of Distance Disengaged

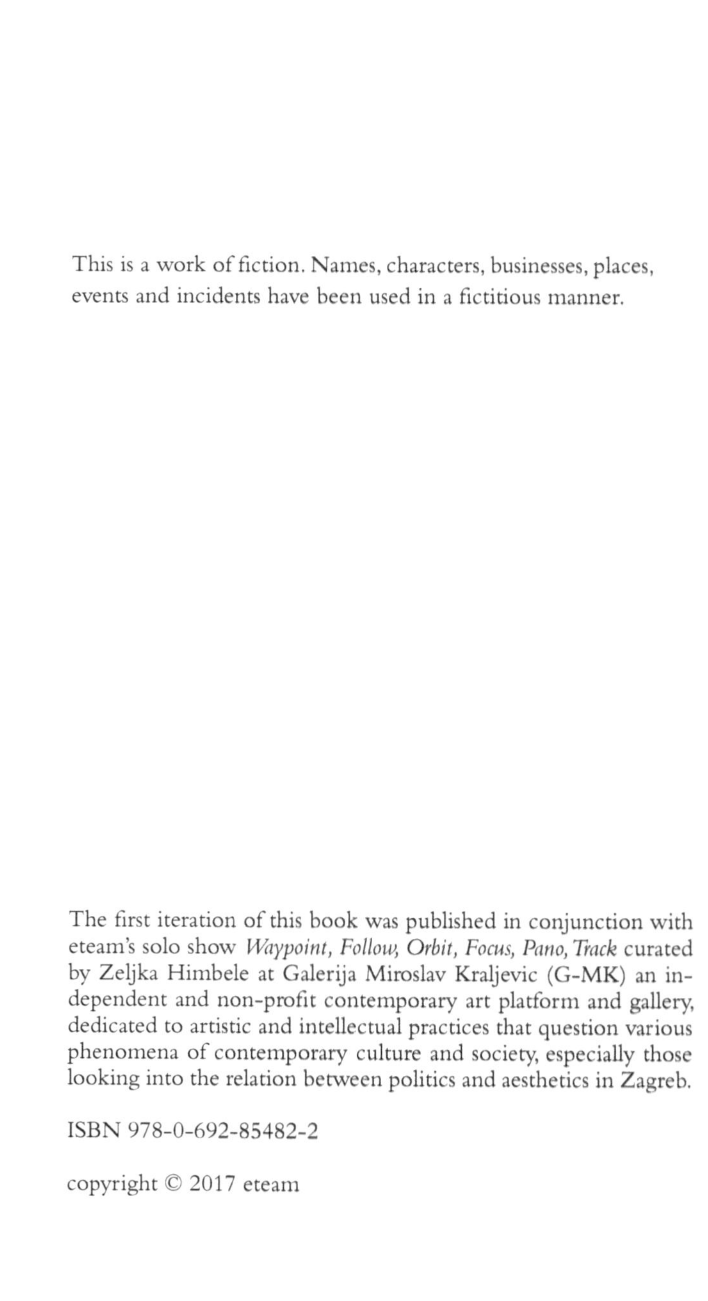

This is a work of fiction. Names, characters, businesses, places, events and incidents have been used in a fictitious manner.

The first iteration of this book was published in conjunction with eteam's solo show *Waypoint, Follow, Orbit, Focus, Pano, Track* curated by Zeljka Himbele at Galerija Miroslav Kraljevic (G-MK) an independent and non-profit contemporary art platform and gallery, dedicated to artistic and intellectual practices that question various phenomena of contemporary culture and society, especially those looking into the relation between politics and aesthetics in Zagreb.

ISBN 978-0-692-85482-2

We are interested in chasing disappearances, we had written in our proposal to the Ministry of Culture to travel to Croatia, want to understand what proves a disappearance, want to figure out if objects, people, places, and countries that have disappeared exist as something else other than an awareness gap in our consciousness. We need to visit Kruku, we had written, need to talk to the designers of the company that develops and produces the camouflage battle dresses for Croatian soldiers and ask how it happened that in 2005, when a new series of three pixilated camo designs intended for army deployment in temperate and woodland, desert and urban scenarios was introduced, the shape of Croatia was incorporated into the pattern.

The Case of Distance Disengaged takes the reader on a mesmerizing, poetic journey through the post-war Balkans, a region whose past and the not-yet of its future move closely alongside the present. Lucid and dreamy at once, *Distance Disengaged* follows visual and cultural clues in search of an ever-elusive culprit: human perception. How do we see (this part of) the world? How do we see ourselves? How does (this part of) the world see us? Weaving together suspenseful adventure with exquisite cerebral meanderings, *Distance Disengaged* opens up new possibilities for historical narrative, storytelling, and documentation, ultimately leading the reader through a most satisfying investigation of the tangle of reality and perception. – Hillit Zwick

eteam is a pair of visual artists who traffic in transience. At the intersection of relational aesthetics, the internet and land art, eteam coordinates collective happenings and conceptual transactions between the earthly plane and the realms of the interweb, often reconstructed in hypnotic video work, radio plays, or more recently novellas and novels. Their projects have been featured at museums and film festivals internationally. They were residents at the CLUI, Taipei Artist Village (TAV), Eyebeam, Smack Mellon, Yaddo and the Mac Dowell Colony and have received grants from Art in General, NYSCA, NYFA, Rhizome, Creative Capital and the John Simon Guggenheim Memorial Foundation.

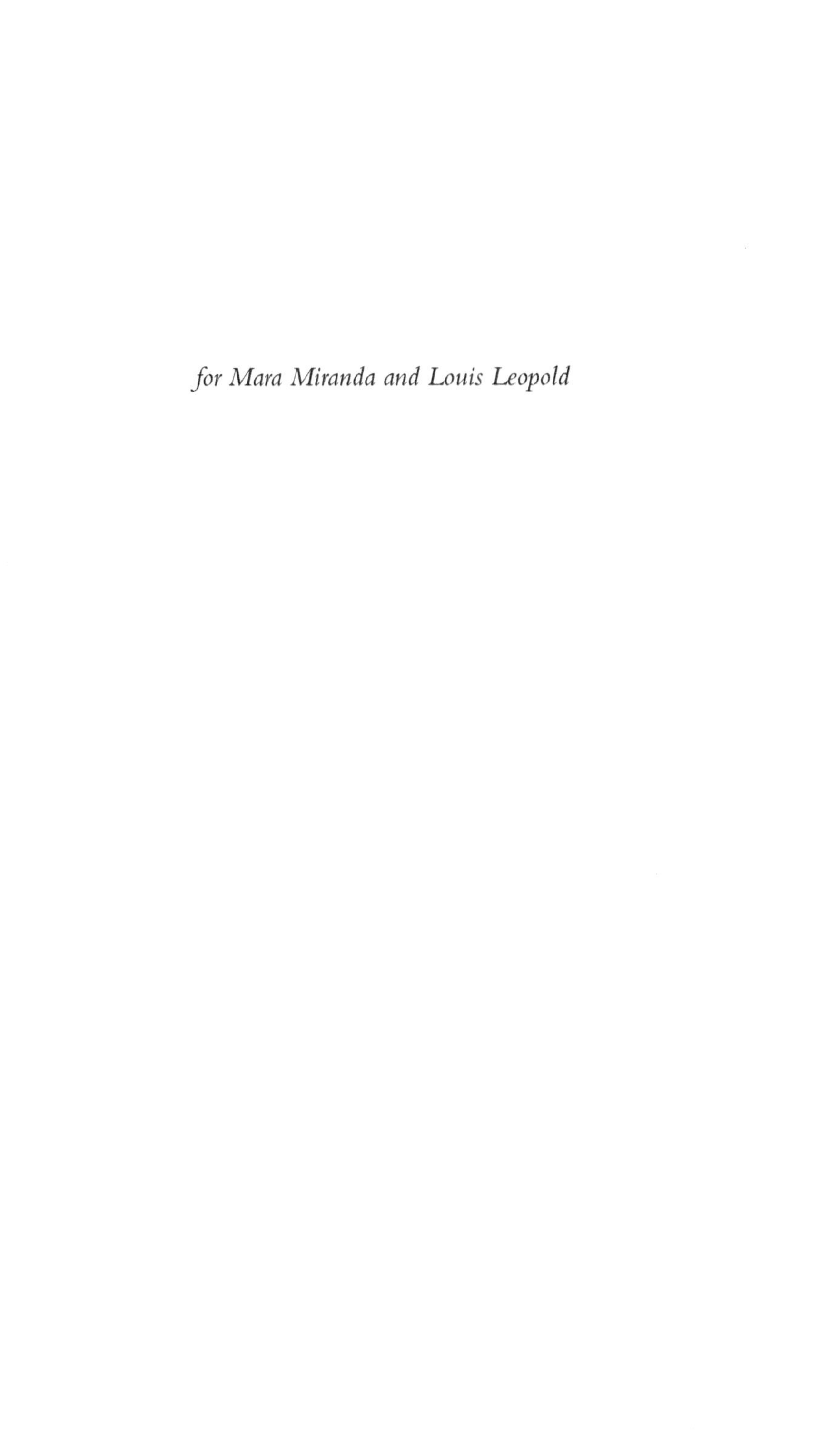

for Mara Miranda and Louis Leopold

Since the war between 1991 and 1995 that separated Croatia from Serbia, a part of our brains automatically links Zagreb with Belgrade. It's the same part that links Germany with Nazi Germany, South Africa with Apartheid, Rwanda with genocide, and the Balkan Wars with war rape, generalized word combinations that trigger generalized images like those of an abandoned brick house on a dirt road in the countryside, a ruin overgrown with the dry remains of an annual vine, missing the glass in its windows and half of its red-tiled roof.

We are willing to picture the place, we think as our plane approaches the city of Zagreb on Saturday July 3, 2016, but we refuse to picture the action, refuse to realize war rape as anything else but a system, an official war strategy employed to achieve ethnic cleansing by gang-raping thousands of women until they became pregnant by the opposing ethnic group.

It only happened twenty-five years ago, a quarter of a century, we realize as we wait in front of three elevated glass boxes containing two men and a woman in uniform. Red passports in hand, we are the last ones of the group that has spilled out of the bus, which has brought us from the aircraft across the airfield to this airport transfer hall. We wait. The line moves slowly. When we exited the aircraft earlier, step-by-step in single file through the front door, and went down the rolling staircase, we only had *one* choice. When we entered the bus, through either the front or the back door, we had *two* choices; and now we have *three* choices, three lines in front of three glass boxes, and we wish we had none. What if we made the wrong decision? Chose to wait in line in front of the wrong glass box?

We are intimidated by immigration officers, border guards, state troopers, city cops, the Feds; we are paranoid driving on a highway in the dark; we become irrational at passport controls. What guarantees that they are following the law? Nothing. What guarantees that the highway continues beyond what is visible in the headlights of a car? Nothing. What guarantees that there is a country behind that passport control station? Nothing. We grew up in a country that doesn't exist anymore, hence we rely on the moon. The moon is a reality—we are willing to agree on that, willing to believe that it has and most likely will continue to transcend what the last generation has built and the next one destroyed, willing to accept that the moon will appear full once a month. It is naïve, even dangerous to take for granted that man-made things like countries, border crossings, citizenships and highways follow a natural trajectory, we say, as we keep our eyes on the Caucasian male who has been issued a uniform and a stool in a glass box in order to regulate the movement of civilians into the Republic of Croatia, a sovereign state located in Central and Southeast Europe, bordering Hungary to the northeast, Serbia to the east, Bosnia and Herzegovina to the southeast, Montenegro to the southeast, the Adriatic Sea to the southwest, and Slovenia to the northwest. What happens if the officer in the glass box doesn't like the way we look? Our faces, our names, our ages, our genders, our dates of birth, our places of birth? What happens if he doesn't like the way we think?

With the little book that certifies her identity and nationality for purpose of international travel in his right hand, the officer looks at an elderly woman in front of him. He then nods and passes the passport back to her through the slit in the glass box. She takes it and steps to the side. He nods again. We wonder if the officer is Croatian, if he is a Croat, and what that would actually mean, besides him possibly cheering for the men in red and white checkerboarded uniforms that make up the Croatian soccer team.

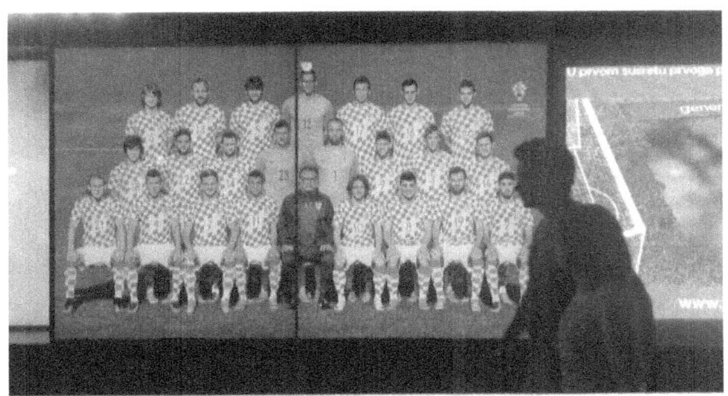

A man steps up, hands him his passport. Its cover is dark green. Is that a good sign or a bad sign, the dark green cover? The officer opens the document. He looks at the open page. Nothing is neutral. There are no neutral colors. This is a green passport. What takes him so long? The man in front of the glass box wears sneakers and jogging pants and a white T-shirt. His arms are muscular. The officer shuffles to another page. The man has more muscles than the officer—that might work against him now, we think. The officer inspects a new page. The man has had more girlfriends, we think. The officer only had three. The last one he would still like to hold authority over. We struggle. We need to stop. We need to figure out a better way to cope with situations in which a seemingly random individual in a state uniform exercises control over the future of a civilian person standing in front of him. We can't just think a woman left him for a man with more muscles. The world is more complex than that. The officer looks up and in our direction. We feel hot flashes running through our upper bodies. He smells us from across the room already. We need to switch. Not the line, that would be too obvious now, we realize, but the thoughts concerning the passport officer. The facts. Just the facts. And the law. Focus on the facts and the law. The officer has blue eyes. He has short blond hair. We have blue and red passports, we are dual citizens, twofold characters; our thinking has been trained to rely on contradictory processes between opposing sides. We can't pledge allegiance to one of the countries, as this would be a betrayal to the other country. We are hybrid products of the binary world, a male and a female, two bodies waiting in a line to be processed.

Outside the airport building stands a white bus destined for Zagreb center. We are told that it will leave in thirty-five minutes.

"How much is a taxi to the center of Zagreb?" we ask the tall man with the post-socialist bent in his back.

"Too much," he says. "Take the bus."

We are concerned, we say to the man, about putting our drone into the belly of the bus and point toward the big black hard-shelled backpack that looks like a casket for an infant. A deep inhalation of cigarette smoke pulls his shoulders into a shrug while he looks at the line where the pavement meets the sky. We clutch the drone closer to our chests, step into the bus, and offer the bus driver a freshly exchanged bill of Croatian currency in exchange for a ticket. He declines by turning his head away from us. We sit down in the second row to the right.

Idleness.

We close our eyes, then we open them. We get out our phone for which we have bought an unlimited data contract, look at the time, start reading the Wikipedia entry for Croatia, look at

the time again, look out the window, push the drone a mil-
limeter further into the middle. Time in an airport bus pro-
ceeds slower than on a plane. It's been thirty minutes already,
and since the conclusion of the Croatian War of Independence,
tourism has grown rapidly—more than eleven million tourists
come to Croatia each year, it says.

We look out the window again. Two men in passport-check-
ing uniforms approach the bus. They are openly disarmed. Instead of guns, they hold civilian cotton bags in their hands;
instead of authority, they carry weariness on their faces. They
take the bus to get home from work, we think, and when they
enter the vehicle, our brains do an imaginary X-ray scan of
their cotton bags. Hard materials appear as blue. Orange is bio-
logical material. Green is for stuff where the density is not great
enough to make it blue or black. The colors in combination
with the outlines of the objects let us draw our conclusions.
A spoon, a fork, an empty plastic container, a metallic water
bottle, a plastic comb, and a newspaper: the benign banality of
the contents of their bags matches the states of their minds. Or
is it the other way around? Their fatigue is infectious, heavy,
and sad, and once they sit down and close their eyes right next
to us, the proximity to the off-duty officers prompts our minds
to produce an animated lullaby of eleven million tourist faces
staring through a bullet-proof window, slowly morphing into
one big holographic question mark.

The bus driver gets up from his seat, walks toward the back, and then slowly, without saying much, makes his way to the front selling tickets. Finally. We are ready to leave. The bus driver sits down in the driver's seat and looks to the right. The door closes and then the vehicle moves forward about five meters, where we come to a stop. There is an automated tollgate one has to pass before leaving the airport, and it looks as if the taxi driver in front of our bus doesn't have the right ticket for the tollgate to open. The taxi driver tries several times to enter a piece of paper into a yellow metal box, but the tollgate stays closed. He slowly backs up, in tandem with the bus, which backs up too. When the bus stops, the taxi driver moves forward, then he turns backward to the right, very slowly and carefully squeezing his vehicle between the bus and the curb to the sidewalk, making it impossible for either vehicle to reach the gate. From our point of view, slightly elevated, it's not clear why he does that. The maneuver becomes even more elusive when he opens his door and tries to exit, as the passage he left between his car and the bus is big enough for a slippery carp to slide through, but not his body. The woman who sits in front of us suggests that he should exit through the passenger door, whereas her companion says that the seat seems to be occupied by a customer, probably a relative of the woman, who sits behind the driver. We look at the presumed relative, who is looking straight ahead. The puffy parts of her hair have been dyed and blow-dried with equal parts skill and hairspray in an old-fashioned beauty parlor. Mrs. Bouffant, we think. Mrs. Bouffant, we repeat. Mrs. Bouffant, the post-Yugoslavian version of Brigitte Bardot. Nothing happens for a while, until the bus driver announces with one clear honk that he will now relax his body, moving from the alert position of a driver into a the comfortable one of an audience member watching a play from an armchair.

Idleness.

Our toes start rubbing each other and then they stiffen, when a male officer steps through the sliding doors of the airport terminal and lights a cigarette. He is the one whose blue, state-employed eyes had, about seventy minutes ago, scanned the features of our faces and compared them with the flattened unlikeness in our passports while we had tried to stop ourselves from flipping through a photo stack of his ex-girlfriends. Everyone has their own defense mechanisms to deal with oppressive moments that come with state-issued authority, yet what about ours? An imaginary stack of good-looking ex-girlfriends who show the male officer the middle finger? That's how we greet authority? We cringe.

The officer steps up to the passenger window of the taxi, slightly bends forward, and then steps back. This is not his territory. The taxi driver needs a ticket that he can feed into the slit of the yellow box, and not a stamp that gets inked on a page in a passport. He walks away and blows cigarette clouds into the air. The gate stays closed, and we apologize to him for speculating about his personal life. Sorry, we say through the window. The bus driver sits still. The taxi driver sits still. Mrs. Bouffant behind him spreads out her ten fingers in midair and looks at her nails. They are painted red. It makes us think of a white towel that is soft and smells like laundry detergent. Someone honks behind the bus. The taxi driver looks in the back mirror and moves his car an inch forward. For the second time, he tries to exit the car, acts out his misfortune with such clumsiness, a few people on the right side of the bus start laughing. We wonder if he could escape by climbing on the roof. No. The taxi driver squeezes back into the car, sits down, and closes the door.

We should use this time, we think, taking out our phone and scrolling through our offline dictionary. *Pre-posterousness, die Abenteuerlichkeit, die Groteskheit, completely contrary to nature, reason, or common sense; absurd; senseless; utterly foolish. Ponderousness, die Gewichtigkeit, of great weight, heavy, massive, dull, labored.* We always wanted to learn a few more words in English. Now would be a good time to practice, we think, and look out of the window again.

Right behind the taxi is a drain hole covered with a metal

grate. An elderly woman with short hair, black, sturdy sandals, dark blue cotton pants, and a big bulky lavender cotton shirt whose trimmings match her pants walks toward it. A laminated card, clipped onto a yellow ribbon and strapped around her neck with a little metal snap hook, dangles over her chest. In her right hand is a broom. Once she reaches the drain, she rubs the metal grate with it, back and forth and back and forth, in order to free it, we reason, from the dust clusters that have attached themselves to its bristles.

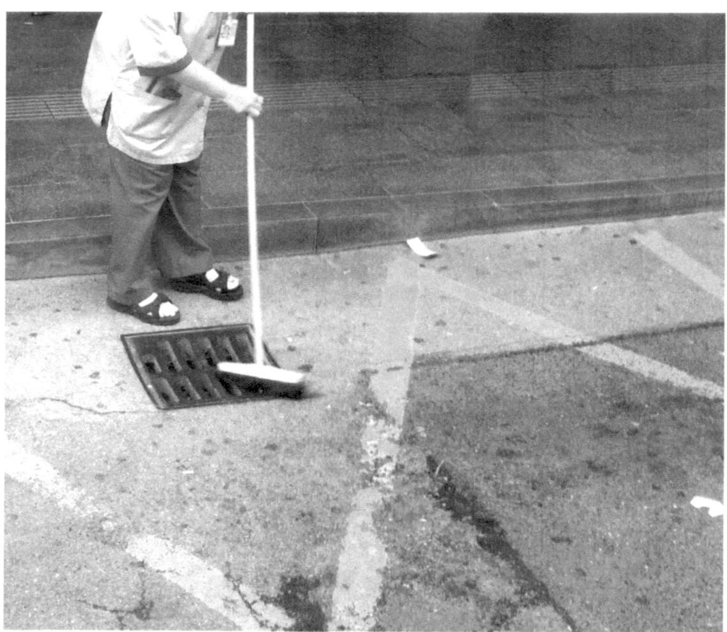

The wondrous workings of the universe, we think. The *hole*, we think, that hole right there next to the bus, created only a few minutes earlier by our boredom, by our anxiety, by our aimless negativity, by our ungrounded speculations, gets now filled by the purpose of the woman who has stepped out of a building to rub off the dust clusters hanging on the bristles of her broom by rubbing the broom on the metal grate of a drain.

We thank the woman. *Thank you*, we say. The world is positive when it is productive, we think, and the cleaning lady embodies that. It is part of her profession, part of her routine, part of her personality, part of her heritage, part of her income. She is part of that perpetuating principle that makes her exist right now as a wondrous reality of this world, as the wonder of the cleaning lady who has dust clusters on the bristles of her broom which she needs to get rid of despite the taxi driver being stuck just two meters in front of her, despite the row of people on the bus laughing about the taxi driver, despite the refugee crisis, despite climate change, despite the fact that two weeks ago, on June 16, 2016, Croatia's parliament voted over-whelmingly to oust Prime Minister Tihomir Orešković only five months after he was elected, an act that is said to keep the government busy with political bickering instead of rebuilding an ailing economy.

Fifty minutes. Fifty minutes have passed since we have en-tered the bus.

Adjacent to the outer wall of the airport building on two con-crete benches, we realize now, sit eight people: six men and two women who are watching what's going on with the closed toll-gate. The benches look futuristic, in a seventies kind of way—concrete casts bent forward into a technological reality where gravitational rules of structural engineering could convincing-ly be considered overcome, were it not for the ninety-degree solidness of the people sitting on them. We are here to stay, their body language seems to say. Comfortably compact, with guarding arms crossed in front of big chests and breasts, they

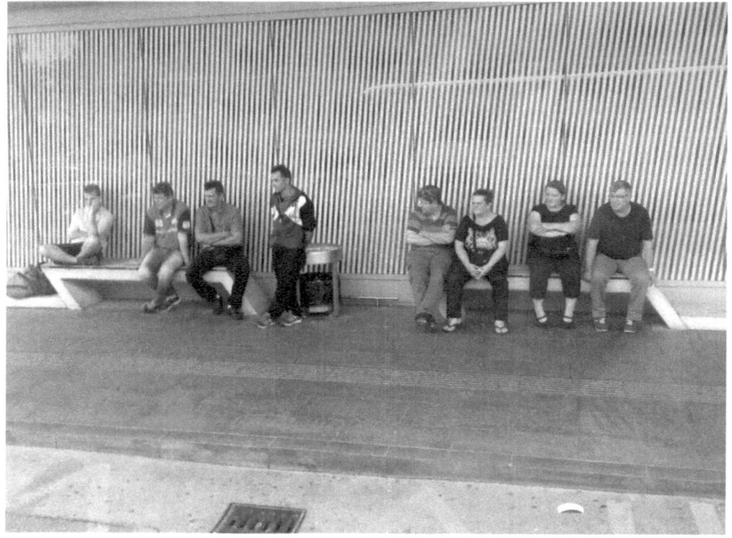

sit, one next to the other, slightly bent forward, amused by the effects the closed tollgate has been producing in front of them.

We think about the word *mass. Massive. Masses,* try to picture *the iron band of terror and ideology* that has the power to chain, according to Hannah Arendt, all men into *One Man.* Totalitarianism, she said, was only possible in societies in which the classes have dissolved into masses and where the responsibility of being an individual citizen has been replaced with the apathy of being a part of a mass. But what is a *human mass?*

We look at the people on the bench again. The ways the thighs of the women interact with the surface are the ways our grandmother's heavy thighs interacted with the bench when she peeled collectively farmed potatoes and snipped peas out of their communist shells. Yet she wasn't *apathetic.* She was *stoic.*

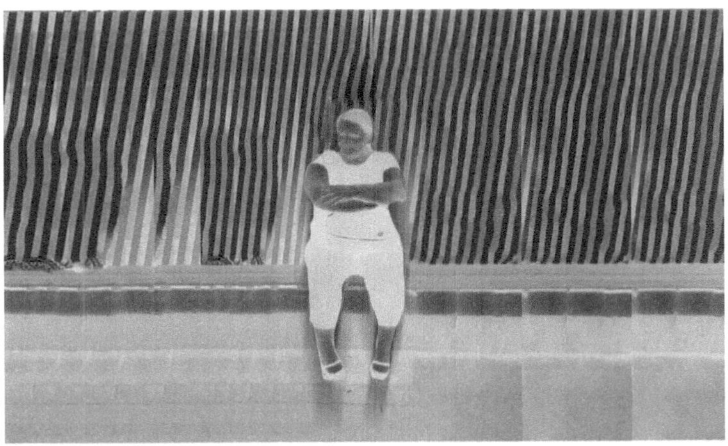

Her life manifested in physical work, she got up at five o'clock in the morning and did housework, then went on to old widows' houses to deliver food and flowers, scrub their floors, wash their bodies, change their diapers. Outwardly free from passion but also unmoved by grief and suffering, she submitted herself without complaint to the unavoidable necessities she found among the forgotten and neglected and never charged a penny. There was no *why*, there were no words, her body was the answer to every question that existed—her big, round body constituted the workings of the world, her moving body was present as the counterweight to our grandfather's constantly questioning, revolting, and meandering brain mass that kept spiraling through the universe. While she cooked rabbits, beans and potatoes our grandfather read Marx, Engels and Lenin in order to prove how easily *exploitable* she was, along with the rest of the uneducated proletarian mass. How did that make her feel? we wonder. *Heavy*, we think. It must have felt very *heavy*. *Heavy like the whole big world she was.*

A slim man in black pants and leather shoes bends down at the passenger window of the taxi, takes some money, and leaves. He looks like a waiter, the way he takes the money. Someone told him to do this. Someone inside the terminal told the waiter to go out there, get the money from the taxi driver, buy a ticket, walk to the gate, and insert a ticket into the slit of the metal box. The gate opens. Just like that. Who knew? The people on the bus cheer. The bus driver gets in position and maneuvers the vehicle through. But wasn't that the taxi driver's ticket, we wonder, and picture how right behind us, as the taxi driver attempts to leave the perimeters of the airport on this gray, rainy Sunday, the gate closes again.

Overspread. Overcast, the condition of the sky when more than ninety-five percent is covered with clouds, we say as we settle into a stare that blurs the peripherals passing by outside the windows of the bus into a bleary flatness surfaced with grass, gravel, and concrete, a stretch of earth with a vague attitude toward an urban, historical density called Zagreb, a place we have never been to. The highways are narrow and lined with metal lampposts that seem incredibly high—so high in fact, that, for a moment, we become concerned about the delay with which their light will hit the asphalt at night.

We keep driving. We keep being driven. We sit still while being moved. Thank you, we say to the bus driver. Thanks for being the bus driver. And thank you for the road.

Zagreb is a pleasant sounding word, we think. Sahhgreb. The sound of the letters, *Zaahhgreb*, the way they lightly buzz on our tongues, zzzzahhh, we repeat the word, keep repeating the acoustics of this European municipality—Zah—greb, Sah--hgreb, sahh-greb, sah-grebh, Tza-grebb, tsahgreb, Saah-grebh—until the word spreads and forms an invisible shape that we are able to grasp with something other than our five senses. Sahhgreb—two open arms that close in with a hug. We come to a stop. On the right side of an intersection, where the driver yields the right of way to oncoming traffic, is a mound of earth shaped like an oversized turtleback. It's covered with rings of bright red and white impatiens. We assume that the few blue ones, which break up the red and white ringlike pattern, are placed in the group to depict a capital letter in an old English font, or the crown of a lion, or something like that, but due to the low resolution that comes with the flower petals, it is hard to tell. The outer perimeter of the mound are lined with a pink ribbon that culminates in a bow. We wonder what the ribbon is made of. It looks like a heavy piece of plastic. Is it linoleum? A bow made of linoleum? They made a linoleum bow around a heap of dirt, we say. They planted flowers on a heap of dirt and put a linoleum bow around it, we say. While the earth was dying, someone drew a circle on the ground, got a truck with dirt, dumped the dirt and raked it round, and put a pink bow around it. Wow, we say. Wow!

According to the directions on our phone, it takes forty-two minutes to walk from the bus station to the accommodations that the women from the gallery have booked for us in advance. Since our suitcases have wheels and most of our funding for the trip has been canceled last-minute due to austerity measures taken by the government, we skip buying a bus ticket or calling a taxi. We pull the metal handles out of the suitcases and walk down Avenija Marina Držića toward two lanes of on-coming traffic. To our left is a parking lot; further to the right, the tracks of a tram, separated from the street by green hedges trimmed into elongated cubes.

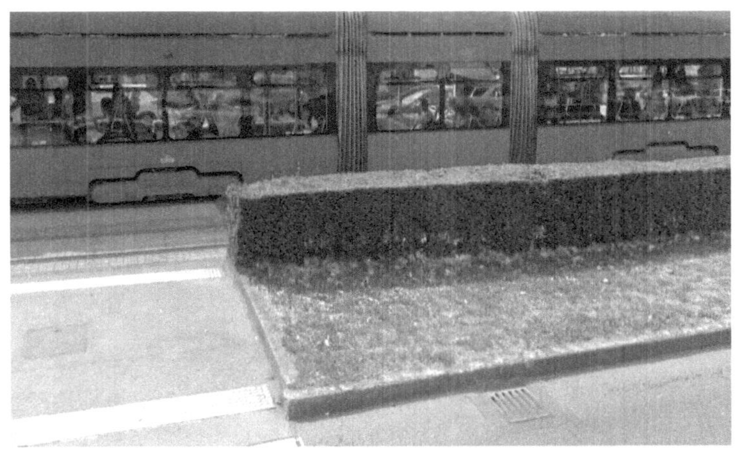

We walk toward an underpass, a steel structure covered with several coats of blue, and cross a wide street. There is a crudely pruned sycamore tree on the other side of the intersection, and a row of small food-stands, some with awnings, some with pieces of mirrored glass, some with graffiti, some with little stairs going up to take-out windows, but all of them closed. It's Sunday, we say, stop, take a deep breath of air and car exhaust, and look around. On the other side of the street is something strangely dignifying, a building with a red-shingled roof and a slim step-out balcony—on its way to attend its own funeral. Greetings, Your Old, Calming Grayness. Thank you for decaying solemnly, we say as we picture a funeral with a group of mourners dressed in black, people in black suits and dresses with lowered heads, us among them, people with black polished shoes, who talk to each other in low voices, until suddenly a tall, skinny waiter with a silver tray appears to serve American Cheez Doodles and nobody can be sad or serious anymore. This is how we laugh, we say, and only with you, Your Old Gray Calmness. And only at your funeral.

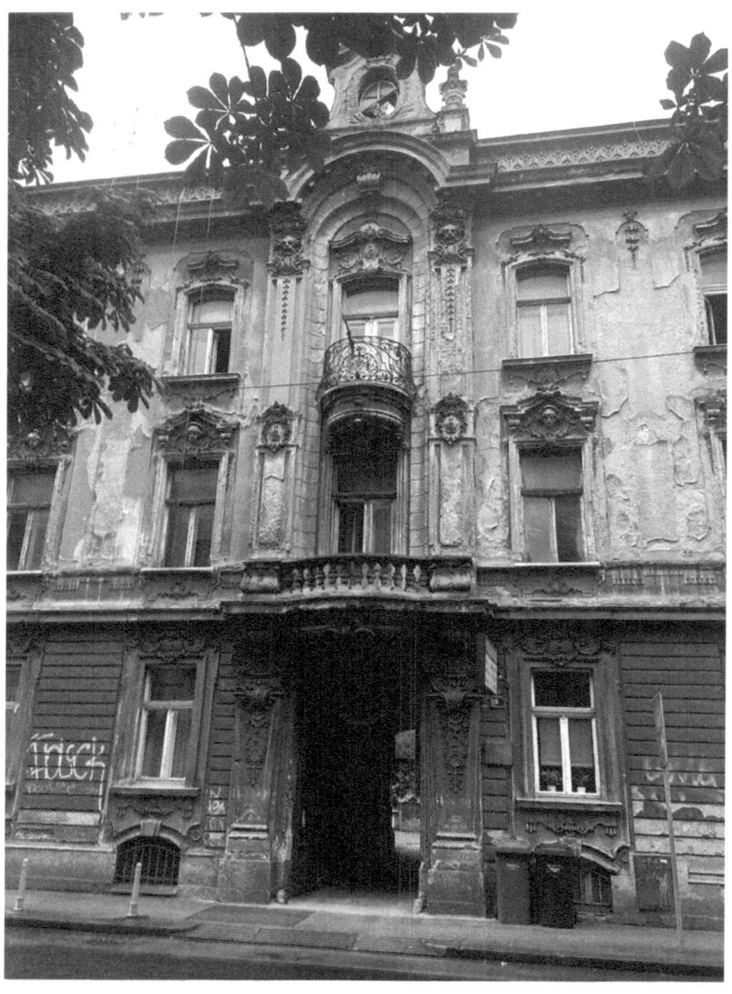

The apartment is in a formerly modest rear building, behind a formerly glorious one. The man in light green shorts who rents *the palace*, as the room is advertised online, according to the women from the gallery, vibrates through the inner court-

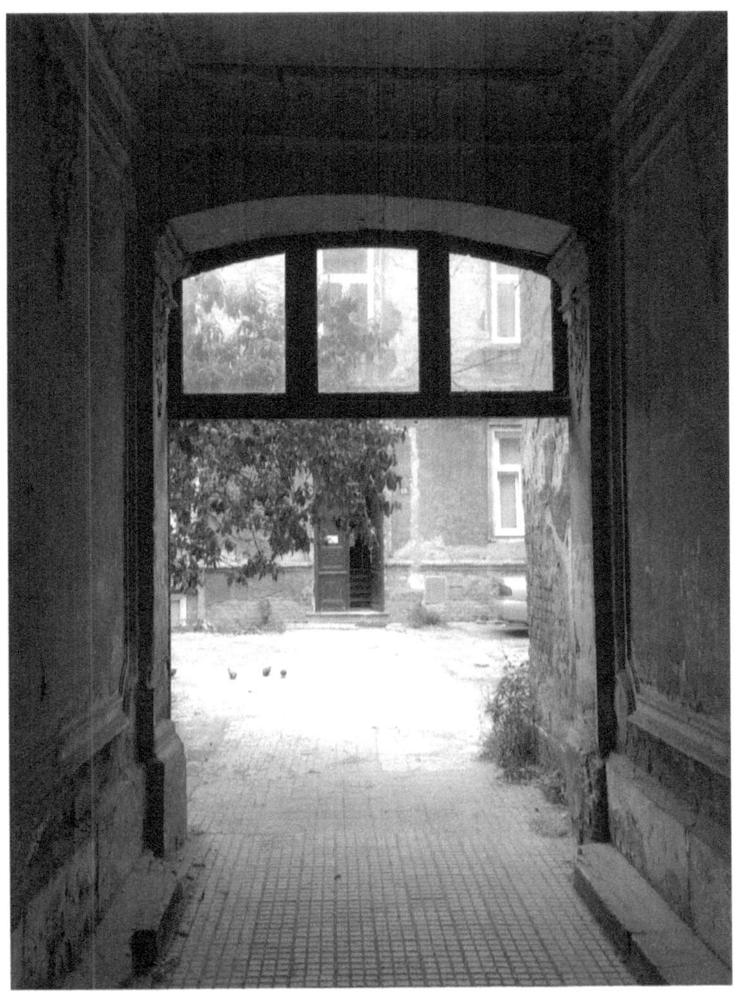

yard with the stiff, nervous pulse of a techno dancer, and is followed by a girl in a light pink dress and white sandals, who is probably eight or nine years old. We can tell they have been waiting for us so the man could give us the keys. One hour, two hours, three hours? We smile at the child, but there is no way to get friendly now. We ruined her Sunday afternoon. We don't even feel apologetic. That's what adults do, we think. This is how the grown-up world works. As long as there are adults around, there has never been and never will be a reasonable Sunday in a kid's life. Adults are being told what to do all week at their jobs, so that on Sundays they don't know what to do on their own, except destroying children's afternoons. It's like that in Germany, it's like that in the United States of America, and it most likely is like that in Croatia, we want to tell the child, while the bobbing man, most likely her father, opens the door to the apartment with an old-fashioned silver key so we can enter a hallway. To the left is the bathroom that we will share with a family who lives behind the closed door in front of us, the man says. To the right, behind the tall, white door with a brass handle, is our room. It is furnished with a black metal bed, whose mattress is covered with a pink polyester sheet. There is an Asian paper screen hiding a corner of the room, a small table and a chair, a wooden nightstand, a lamp whose bulb is dangling from its shell, and a hole in the floor. We open the new double-paned plastic window and look out into the inner courtyard.

"Thank you," we say in English, because it hadn't even oc-

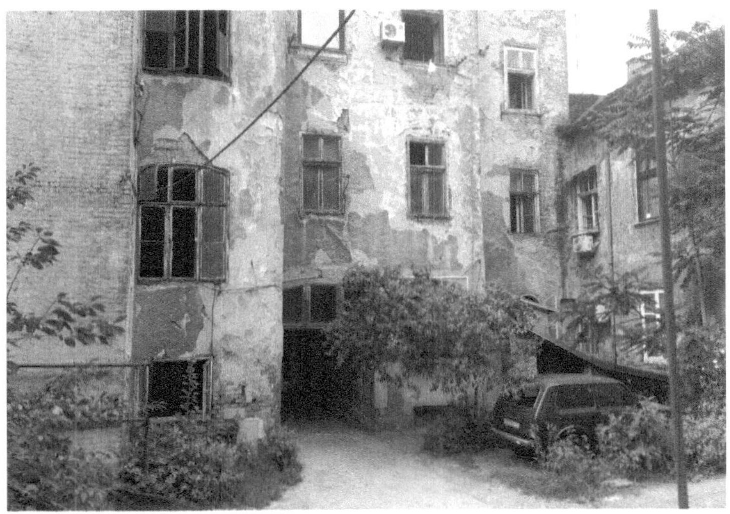

curred to us in the airport bus to learn some Croatian; it hadn't even crossed our minds that instead of advancing our English, we could have also learned some basic Croatian, which makes us feel ashamed a few seconds later, when we watch the man running through the courtyard, the girl behind him.

We keep standing at the window looking out. There is an ash tree and a fig tree, a peach tree, and a white Rose of Sharon bush among some tall, large-leaf weeds, a bunch of red hollyhocks, three parked cars, a regular rose bush, and broken-up patches of tiles between condensed dirt and a few loose pebbles. A broken strip of worn-out yellowish tiles runs from the hallway of the front house to the entrance of the backhouse, slowly fading out in the middle, then picking up momentum again, eventually reaching the entrance to the back door in full formation.

The back facade of the front building has been patched many times, with many different mixtures of sand, cement, and water—some light, some dark, some yellowish, some gray. Some of the windows are made of new white vinyl, their shades are drawn and sealed. They look impenetrable and cold like refrig-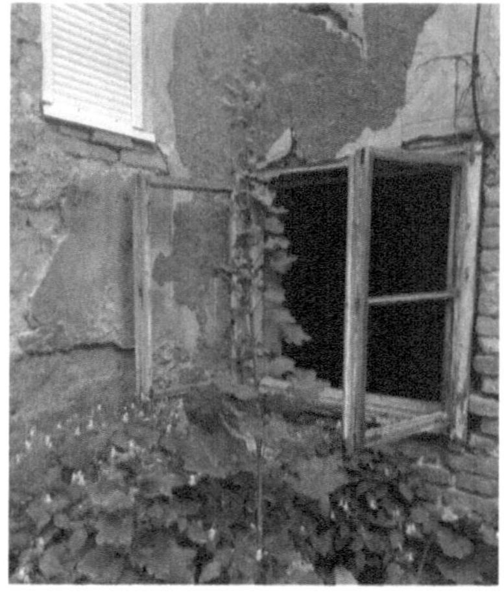erators, especially right next to the old, unpainted, withered, darkened wooden ones, which are mostly open. Open because it is hot outside? Open because they don't close anymore and haven't for years? *Broken*, we think, broken, we say, like the hearts of characters in novels that take place in Eastern Europe.

We text the women from the gallery, telling them that we have arrived. They text back that we should take the blue tram at Marshal Tito Square to the Museum of Modern Art in New Zagreb and ask for Tonka, who will get us in for free and give us a tour. We lock the white door to our room, turn the key to the apartment two times, and enter the hallway that resembles a space in time when the word *home* was still connected with a certain place. The lower half is painted dark green, the upper half is painted white, and each stair's outer edge has been

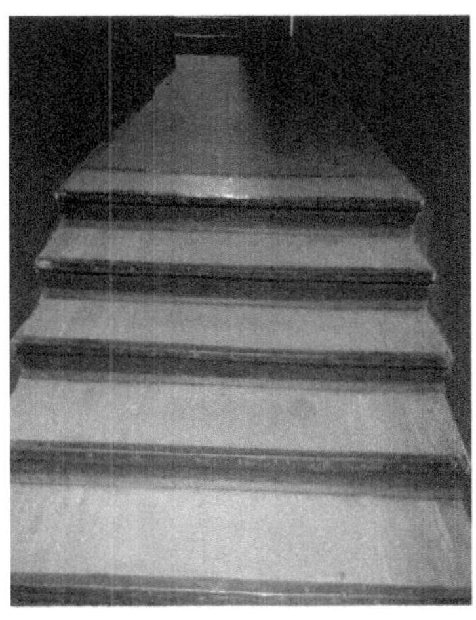

reinforced with a strip of orange copper that is bent and nailed on top of gray linoleum with big-headed nails, like it had been in the five-hundred-year-old house we had lived in in Weimar, where our landlord's seventy-year-old sister, Mrs. Misterman, who, due to her shortness, was the only one who could still live in the five-hundred-year-old servants' quarters under the roof, had first taught us, and then supervised once a week over a period of three years, how to broom, then mop, then dry, and finally wax the staircase in the house that already had, she used to say, been swept, mopped, dried, and waxed in the very same way, since Martin Luther had given his sermons across the street in the Herderkirche.

We step into the courtyard. The peach tree, we realize now, has at least a hundred green peaches hanging on its branches. It looks like a promising harvest, yet we can't refrain from asking the tree a question: How many will ripen to maturity? Eight maybe, or ten if you are lucky, the rest will drop completely pointlessly, we answer, and enter the dark passageway of the front building. There is a staircase that leads to a room with an open door. A man in a black suit stands in front of a copy machine and holds a stack of papers. The room is lit by a neon light. It is a copy shop, we think, they still have *copy shops* in Zagreb, they still have dedicated places for people to go and make physical copies of letter-sized papers. We remember that the word *stereotype* comes from the printing trade and was first adopted in 1798 by Firmin Didot, a French engraver and typefounder,

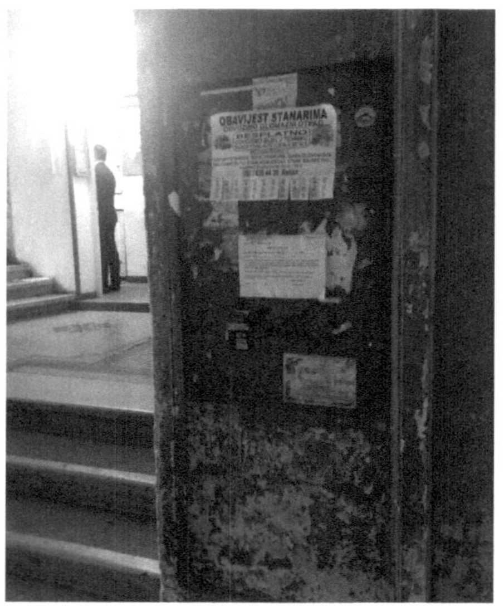

to describe a printing plate that duplicated any typography. *Typefounder,* we think, while the man in the black suit opens the lid of the copy machine and puts a paper on the glass. What these old *stereotypes* have turned into, we think. Would there even be stereotypes without mass-copied written words? Isn't every printed word nothing but a stereotype?

We stand there and look. Our bodies understand the foreign passageway, know how to relate to the sod that has darkened the breaks in the stucco, the peeling parts of paint, the decorative moldings on the ceiling, the curled-up leaves and the hanging nuts, the fanlike shells or feathers among the vines that keep repeating their abstracted swing with mathematical accuracy, the double stucco frames that enclose the emptiness inside themselves and their typical bent corners, the cracks, the fissures, the fractures, the crevices, the dimensions of the hallway, its width, its height, the way the wall has been scratched by strollers and bikes and handcarts and refrigerators that have been carried in and out, the smell of coal and car exhaust, the moistness of damp dust, the arch of the ceiling, the arch of the window above the door that is missing, the graffiti and the brown metal mailboxes that have been banged and stuffed and jammed and locked and emptied, the stone steps that shine where they have been stepped on most often, the way the light falls onto the worn-out tiles from the back and through the half open door from the front. We take in everything without even thinking about it, until the light switch next to the staircase interrupts the flow and commands our mental attention with some unpleasant urgency, signals somehow, within the means available to a light switch, that it is dangersome not to pay attention to its position on the wall.

What is it about the light switch? we ask. The light switch stands out, we say, the light switch sits outside the normal parameters of a naturally decaying passageway, the light switch is

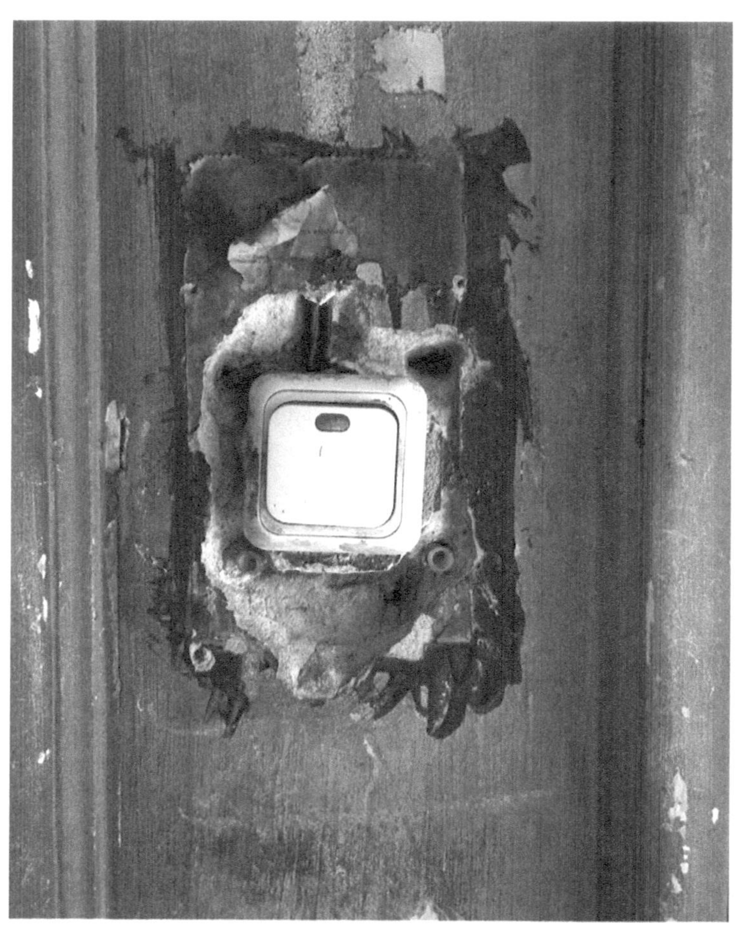

an open wound that is bleeding, the light switch doesn't have the conviction to conceal that it is embedded in a violent act of the past—yet, it's actually not the light switch that makes us uncomfortable, we say, but the hole around it. That hole is offensive, we say, it is a dumb, dirty hole that houses the light switch. That hole is real, the senseless result of some primitive aggression when the wall was violated by some rude, unskilled person, who got angry when the anchors for the screws started wobbling the moment he hammered them in, and the plaster chipped off, and the bricks got loose. Why is there *paper* behind the plaster, packaging paper with decoratively trimmed edges and words typed on with a typewriter? we ask as we step closer. It's actually two pieces of paper, we now realize, old brown pieces of paper partly covered with typewriter-written words. One is lighter, one is darker, we say, like the pieces from Kennedy's autopsy report, typed out with a typewriter on paper that has darkened now. The meticulous bureaucracy that comes with official violence sits in those holes in form of paper, we say, and feel how they draw us into the tunnel from where we enter the path *the magic bullet* had taken when the president of the United States of America was assassinated on November 22, 1963, in Dallas, Texas, by a three-centimeter-long copper-jacketed lead core 6.5x52mm Mannlicher-Carcano rifle bullet, which had struck his well-built, well nourished Caucasian body in the back and exited through his throat and then went on flying through the limousine toward Texas Governor John Connally, who sat in front of the president.

It's hard to believe, we say, the same bullet that had already traveled through the back and the neck of President Kennedy, then entered Connally's back, exited through his chest, and passed through his wrist to finally embed itself in the Governor's thigh, on its way traversing fifteen layers of clothing, including a necktie knot, seven layers of skin, and approximately fifteen inches of tissues, shattering a radius bone and removing a total of four inches of rib. Remember that passage in the Warren Commission report? The beauty of paper is the ability to peel back the layers and go back and forth in time, we say, yet if there is a truth, then the truth of this building sits *between* the typed-on paper and the four holes that surround this light switch. The light switch has potency to be a deadly sign, we say, someone could be shocked by this light switch, someone could die being touched by this light switch, we say, yet no one will die, because the chances are so incredibly low that we almost get sad about the benign state the light switch has been left with hanging in the wall there, almost feel sorry for this scenario of empty holes and black electricity cable that holds the white rounded plastic square in place. Sorry, we say to the light switch, and fake a little jerk with which we would pull our son away from the light switch if he were with us, when we would caution him, despite its benignity, not to touch this open wound, but rather cross the hallway in the dark.

How did the building get it? he would ask. The building didn't brush its teeth, we would say, now starting to improvise an alternative for a six year old that does not include the assassination of the president of the United States. Bacteria crept in, we would say, started feeding on the leftovers in the crevices and then started eating up the building. Nobody cared until the cavity was deep enough to expose the nerve. It started hurting, the people in the building felt the pain, especially in the middle of the night, so the people cried out and urged the super to notify the nerve doctor and fill the cavity, whereupon the nerve doctor, which in building terms is the electrician, did notify the superintendent that he didn't have the materials to fill in the tooth and heal the pain of the nerve due to a national supply shortage, but still would be glad to take a look at the open wound the next day, since he had to come by the building anyway, in order to make a copy of his response paper to the notification for the superintendent in the copy shop. The next day the electrician would come by, we would say to our son, he would look at the wound and then make a paper copy of his response to the notification from the super. He would file his original notification response into a folder, put that folder back into his brown leather bag, then fold up the copy of the notification response and put it into an envelope, which he would give to the electrician, who would put it into the breast pocket of his blue working jacket. And then the super and the electrician would walk into the inner courtyard and take a little break, and while they smoked a cigarette under the peach tree, the super would tell the electrician how he once saw the super of a big building in south Zagreb run purposefully into a hole in a wall. That man kept running against the wall, the super would say, once, twice, three times, four times, five times, six, seven, eight, until he had turned himself into a bloody pulp with which he attempted to fill the hole in the wall. That's absolutely absurd, the electrician would say. What is absurd? our son would ask.

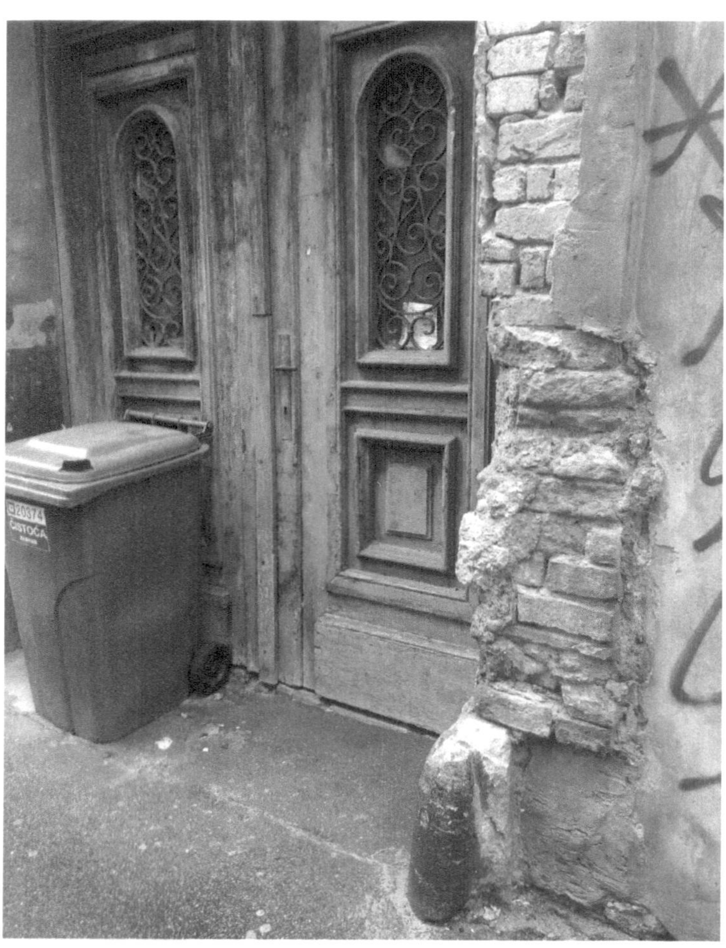

Absurd, we would say, tightly holding his hand while walking east on Andrija Hebrangova toward Marshal Tito Square, are the green plastic trash bins in front of every building you see on this street. Look at them, we would say. They are completely out of tune with everything else that's going on. Look at the buildings. What do you see? Collapsed windowsills, chipped-off corners, dented walls, holes and exposed bricks—yet what is new, clean, and pristine? The trash bins. And what does it tell you? Death is not compatible with the rest of life. Death stands in opposition to life, it is the most common everyday abnormality. Death is as consistently unnatural as these sterile green trash bins in front of the naturally decaying buildings on this street. These trash bins are the vertical coffins that remind us that life is short. Look, we would say to our six-year-old son. At the end of the day, or first thing in the morning . . . What do the people of Zagreb do? They put their stinky discards into a plastic bag, tie it up, and no matter who they are or what they wear, no matter if it's raining or if the sun is shining or what kind of door they open to leave the house or which specific door handle they push down or which knob they turn, their trash ends up in the same dark green generic trash bin as everyone else's. This is why you have to try to love life the way it is and embrace its paradoxes, which should come easy, we would say to our son, especially if it's clearly laid out, like on this street in front of you.

We take the blue tram, which runs, once we cross the river

Salva, in the center of a wide, empty, multilaned boulevard. We go back the same way, we realize now, we had taken two hours earlier toward Zagreb center with the airport bus. Massive, concrete housing blocks are placed— sometimes in groups of three, sometimes in groups of five—in big areas of empty, flattened, antisocial-looking space. The women from the gallery will tell us later that Novi Zagreb is a grand mid-century experiment in utopian city planning, and indeed, passing through we already feel something possibly *grand*, something possibly *utopian*, but it's hard to know where—between the repeating elements of stacked-up concrete into heights that simultaneously dwarf, impress, and depress—one exactly should anchor the human dream of a common future. Socialist, communist, brutalist architecture? Concrete brute? Form follows function? What must have once looked like a modern rupture from the past looks now like a nostalgic breach from the present—a pretentious wordplay that makes us realize that we have actually no idea what we are talking about, that we never lived in a socialist housing block, that we never wanted to, that we were always uncomfortable with the alienating melancholy that automatically attached itself to the annual visits to our aunt's one-bedroom apartment in Berlin-Marzahn, where she would pull out four little stools from underneath a small square plastic laminated kitchen table. We would sit down, she would open a box and unfold a cardboard square with lines, we would choose a color for our game pieces—little soldiers in solid red, green, blue, or yellow—and then we would play Chinese checkers, which was a nice activity, yet *nice* was never something we responded to very well. We never trusted *nice*, nice always felt like neither nor, nice always felt too rational or too neutral, nice always had that algid air around its "c" sound at the end that made us want to leave and run away back to the messy life that in our experience so far had happened along a bunch of dirt paths sprinkled with the poop of animals. Maybe that's why we smile now, we say, looking out the window of the tram at the dirt path that runs diagonally from the tram station across the empty field to one of the housing blocks.

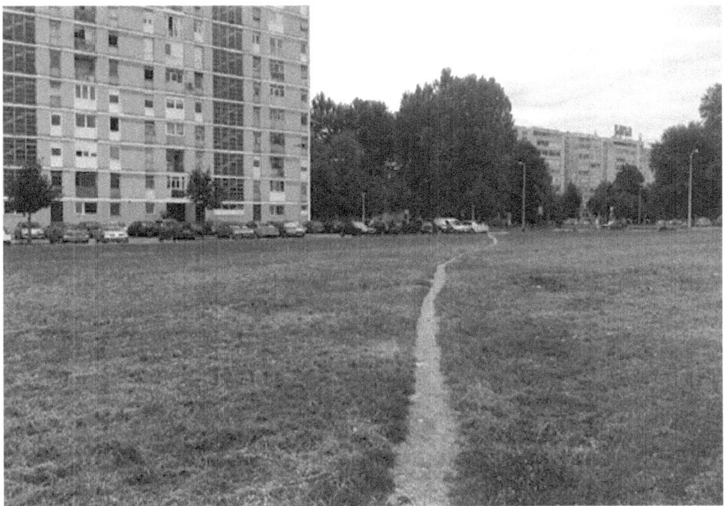

It often takes only a small detail to establish a sense of familiarity in an alienating world, we say. And even if it is only a tiny thing, once recognized, *that thing* becomes the straw to hang on to. It might be just a smell, or the pattern of a fabric, or the way a word is written—the typography of an "m," for example, the "m" that stands for mundane and modern, man and murder. For us, the dirt paths do the trick, we say. *We trust dirt paths.* To us, dirt paths are clear signs. They stand for a population that, despite everything, goes its own ways, hence they are our access roads to Novi Zagreb. We entered Novi Zagreb in a tram *on tracks,* and that meant nothing to us until we saw the dirt tracks, we say. Those dirt paths are precious, we say, not only because they counterbalance the monolithic glory of rectangular, geometric forms, those dirt tracks are telling because they are trampled into the ground *diagonally* by the wisdom of the human herd. Those are the lines of resistance that have been walked by people in ways that hadn't been planned on paper or built with machines; those dirt paths are maintained through the daily walks of people, people who keep adjusting the details that aren't working and have never been working in the state-issued master plan for Novi Zagreb.

At every station another person gets off the tram. Nobody gets on, and eventually it's just us and a woman in the double car. The blue dot on our map on our phone shows that we are close to the museum. The tram stops and the doors open. It doesn't look like an official stop. There is no tram shelter. We stay seated and look at the woman, who looks out the window at a tower block whose structural conformity is disrupted by the ways the residents of the flats have customized their formerly identical balconies using a variety of materials and colors now available in the free market economy. The tram driver comes out of the driver's cabin, looks at us, and then uses both hands to nonverbally communicate with an energetic swing that the doors are open for us to exit. He knew right away we don't speak a word of Croatian, we say as we jump over the tracks and jaywalk across the three lanes of Avenija Dubrovnik.

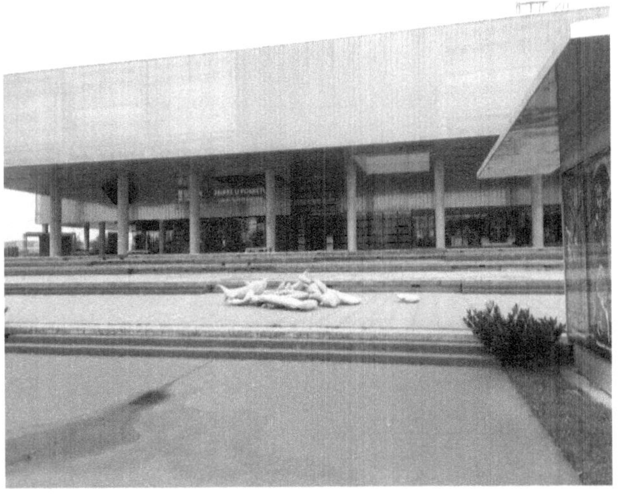

The Museum of Contemporary Art looks modern—modern meaning a mix of concrete and glass that constitutes a big block of architecture that rises with a palpable purpose on unadorned columns above a plaza with stairs and concrete benches. Unfortunately it looks closed, not only today but for quite some time. The women from the gallery must have meant a different museum. There are no people, and there are no lights, thus we jump back when, during our attempt to peek through the glass windows on the ground floor, a sliding door opens automatically. We are startled. The door closes again. We step forward and it opens. We enter a lobby that is dark and in a state of acoustic emergency. We scan the space until we locate a red, blinking, wall-mounted fire alarm notification appliance that's emitting the shrill tone. A male clerk with broad shoulders sits calmly behind the counter. We try to make eye contact in order to figure out if we should come closer or call the fire department, but the clerk leaves that decision completely up to us.

When we reach the counter, we offer a greeting, which the clerk can't hear because of the fire alarm.

"Tonka" we say, noticeably louder.

"You?"

"eteam."

He picks up the stationary phone and speaks quietly into the handset, then hangs up, hands us two tickets, and says we should wait. There is a brochure on the ticket counter. The museum, we read, was opened in December of 2009, six years after the cornerstone was laid in 2003.

"Two thousand and nine?" we say in disbelief.

"But why does it look like it was built in the sixties or seventies?" we will later ask everyone we meet.

"It's a *homage*," people will say with the genuine respect that honors the use of such a word and undertaking.

Eventually the fire alarm turns silent, and shortly after Tonka appears. She walks fast in her elevated silver shoes, speaks fast, and quickly cuts the bullshit with the sharp edge of her asymmetrical haircut when we try to make polite conversation and ask how the permanent collection of the museum is organized:

"It's international, because everything is international these days, and it's not chronological, because nothing is chronological anymore. Take your pick, you have less than an hour."

And then she disappears and leaves us alone with a huge black-and-white photo printout of a young woman in a white tank top who looks straight into the camera lens.

On the wall label we read that the text is graffiti written by a Dutch unknown soldier on an army barracks wall in Potočari, Srebenica, sometime between 1994 and 1995, when the Royal Netherlands

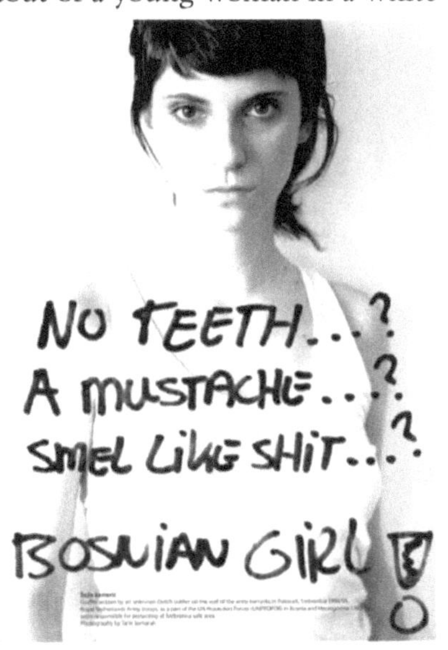

Army troops, as part of the UN Protection Force (UNPRO-
FOR) in Bosnia and Herzegovina from 1992 to 1995, were
responsible for protecting the Srebrenica safe area. The work
is by Šejla Kamerić, a Bosnian artist. We open the first entry
that comes up when we search the internet on our phone for
Srebrenica-Potočari.

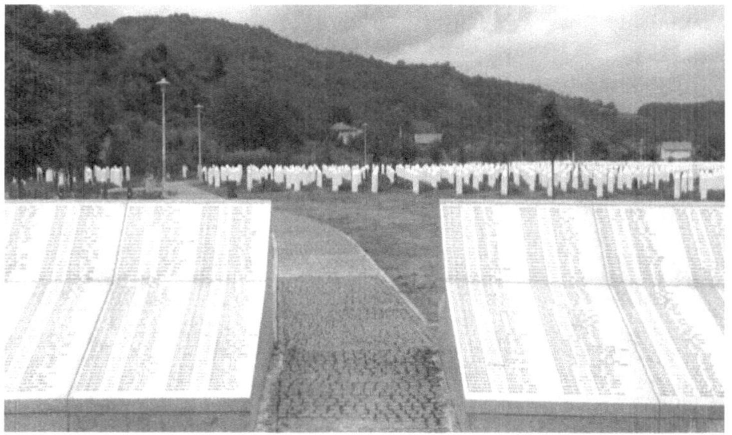

*The massacre in Srebrenica began in Potočari, where some 25,000
Bosniak refugees had desperately gathered awaiting evacuation. After
entering the city in 13 July 1995, Bosnian Serb forces moved into
Potocari and separated many Bosniak men and teenage boys from the
rest of the crowd before killing them; some women and girls were raped
and killed as well. The Dutch UN peacekeepers stationed in Srebrenica were unable to stop the massacre, despite having their headquarters
in the town. In all, about 1,200 innocent people were murdered at
Potocari before the survivors were evacuated to Tuzla.* (Wikipedia)

"Do you remember in 2001, when we had the studio in the 91st floor in the World Trade Center and there was a fire alarm?" we say less than an hour later, walking down Dubrovnik Boulevard toward three tall, identical looking housing towers.

"Yes."

"Remember how we went down the stairs to the street and stood there and watched the truck and its long ladder and the firemen busy pulling hoses and connecting them to the fire hydrants?"

"Yes."

"Remember how that felt appropriate, how it felt the firemen were doing the right thing?"

"Yes."

"We watched for a while. Do you remember that? We got coffee and watched. "

"Yes."

"Looked at the truck and the firemen. The blinking lights on the trucks, the sirens and the air horns as more units were responding, the fire chief talking into a walkie-talkie, a guy pulling the hose, the extended ladder, someone climbing up slowly, climbing higher, fifty feet, seventy feet, one hundred feet."

"Yes."

"And then, suddenly, we looked up to the top of the building. Do you remember that? Do you remember the shock, do you remember how our eyes suddenly filled with tears when we realized the proportions, realized what the fully pulled-out ladder could do in comparison to what it couldn't?"

"Why do you tell this story now?"

"Doesn't the red awning of this coffee bar over there look like the pulled-out ladder of the fire truck?"

"What do you mean?"

"How many people live in this housing block?"

"Eight hundred? One thousand? I don't know."

"And how many chairs are in this coffee bar for people to sit here and have a coffee? How much room has been given to the hundreds and thousands of mothers, fathers, and children residing in these centrally-heated dwellings above this small coffee bar to take a break from cooperating in economics and reproduction? How many of them can actually come down and be *ordinary*, drink a coffee, socialize and integrate their isolated, nuclear family into something like collectively lived life?"

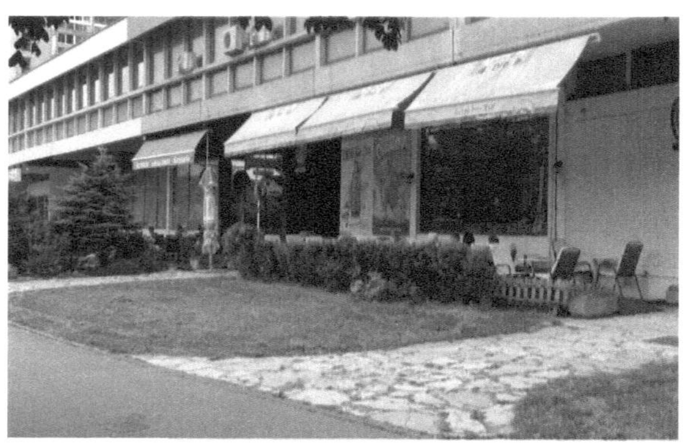

We sit down in the coffee bar on Dubrovnik Boulevard and order two cappuccinos, which come as filtered coffee with heavy cream from a spray can. We look at the few other guests who do not look like fathers, mothers, or children that live together in nuclear families, nor do they look like people who cooperate in economics or reproduction, and then we look at the green outdoor carpet the café is covered with, and then at the cubical green hedge, which separates the café from the sidewalk, until the next hedge separates the sidewalk from Dubrovnik Boulevard, until three lanes later another hedge separates the tracks of the tram from the fast lane on the Boulevard, until two tram tracks later a hedge separates the other side of Dubrovnik Boulevard.

Concrete buildings, a wide empty boulevard, hedges, roses, and a blue tram. Strips of roses between asphalt, corner triangles with roses, a yellow crane in the distance, concrete-cased circles with roses, ovals with roses, traffic islands with roses. *Concrete and roses,* that is the combination of smells and forms and colors that cap-tures an era, we say. European state socialism has done with roses what it has done with concrete. Amazingly good things and pretty

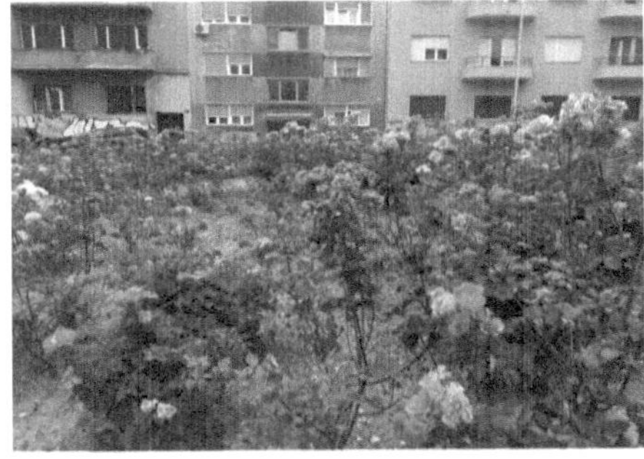

bad things and all the mediocre versions in between, we say.

We love concrete. We really do. If there were one material, we say, we had to use to describe humanity during an aptitude test for art school, it would have to be concrete. The Pantheon in Rome was made out of concrete, we would say to the professors; the Hoover Dam, we would say; bridges, blocks, Brasilia, we would say; St. John's Abbey Church in Minnesota; the bunkers of WWII; the underground bomb shelters; the road blocks; the planters; the stairways; the pillars; the monuments; the basements; the curved and apparently light-weighted, reinforced, daring, utilitarian, rational, radical Russian bus shelters and the American gas station roofs.

We love concrete, we say, stirring the whipped cream with the filtered coffee. As children, we thought it was part of a *magic act* to shovel white sand and gray cement powder into the cement mixer that was so over-used, we say, a thick, hardened crust covered its formerly dark blue metal shell like barnacles or mussels in the Baltic Sea. The mixer was borrowed from the mixer-man and ran on high-powered current, we remember now. The plastic cover of the plug was deteriorated, and because we sometimes missed throwing the water directly into the opening of the whirling womb, and because we had been given explicit descriptions of what happens if a human being gets electrocuted, we always knew that mixing concrete was a complicated miracle for humans to be part of. Maybe that's why we became addicted: addicted to the smell of concrete when it is freshly poured and addicted to the ways it smells in damp basements when mold starts to attach itself and addicted to its surface variations, the rough versions and the polished ones. We see the imprinted wood-grain texture on the finished face of a concrete wall and think of fossils and how they are tens of thousands of years old. We compare that time with the life expectancy of contemporary concrete, and that leads us to think about our lives. How long does generic concrete last? Fifty years, sixty years, seventy years? Maybe it's one of those man-made materials that perfectly parallels the artificiality of an industrial human life that comes with those reinforced strengths and crumbling weaknesses, we say, and that's why we can relate to it. Or maybe we just love the color gray. Maybe our highest ideal is to become neutral and moderated and gray and useful and to do something *concrete*. Remember how we read somewhere that the human eye can't see more than thirty-two shades of gray? At the time it sounded like a reasonable number, we say. That's one shade of gray for every day of the month, we now remember having thought as we had pictured two rows of sixteen squares of darker-getting-whites and lighter-getting-blacks stacked on top of each other. But then we kept reading just to find out that the number of shades of color an average human eye can see is one million. That's hundreds and thousands of blues and hundreds and thousands of greens in contrast to thirty-two shades of gray, we say. That's like having grown up in the East, learning for the first time about the West. It had always been *enough*, until the day our grandmother got an antenna strong enough to receive West German TV and we watched a Spearmint chewing gum commercial.

We leave the coffee bar, walk back toward the tram station, and decide to make the detour and cross Dubrovnik Boulevard in a legal manner by taking one of the pedestrian underpasses that are located at the next intersection. Like the boulevard above, the underpass is grand, and like the Museum of Contemporary Art, it is dimly lit, devoid of people, and filled with art.

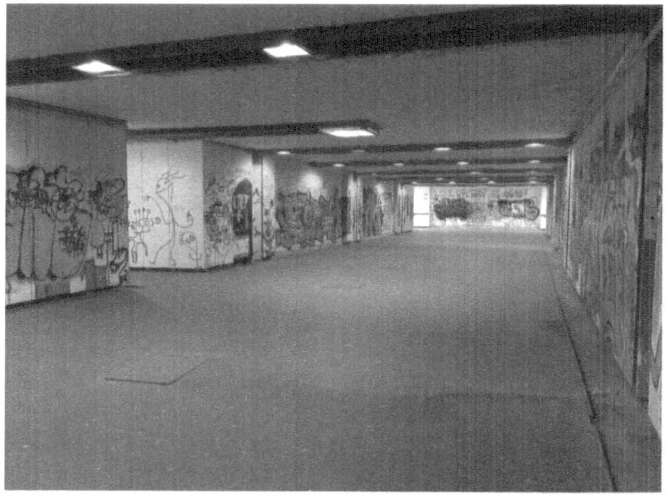

We are interested in chasing *disappearances*, we had written six months earlier in our proposal, "Croatia Camofleur," to get funding from the city of Zagreb and the Ministry of Culture to travel to Croatia and conduct research for a solo show at the not-for-profit gallery G-MK. We want to understand how things disappear and what proves a disappearance, want to figure out if objects, people, places, and countries that have disappeared exist as something else other than an awareness gap or as a substitute in our consciousness. We looked up the word *void* in an online dictionary, we wrote. The first explanation that came up was void as an adjective, void as in law, void as in having no legal force or effect, something that is not legally binding or enforceable—and that made us curious to know if there was a connection between the not enforceable and the fact that the official combat uniforms of the Croatian Armed Forces have integrated into their pixilated camouflage pattern the digitized map of Croatia.

We need to visit Kruku, we wrote in our proposal to the Ministry of Culture, need to talk to the designers of the company that develops and produces the camouflage battle dresses for Croatian soldiers and ask how it happened that in 2005, when a new series of three pixilated camo designs intended for army deployment in temperate and woodland, desert and urban scenarios was introduced, the shape of Croatia was incorporated into the pattern. We are confused, we wrote, and would like to clarify. If the main objective of military camouflage is to deceive the enemy as to the presence, position, and intentions of military formations, if surface patterns are used to conceal or disguise as much information as possible, if camouflage works through dazzle, countershading, and the disruption of outlines, how come the outline that stands out repeatedly in the pattern of the Croatian combat uniform is the shape of Croatia's map?

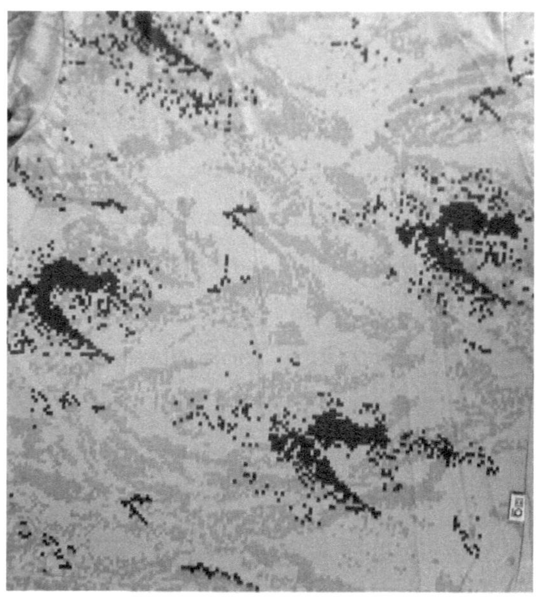

We leave in a rental car on a two-lane highway. The outskirts in this direction are lined with enormous, colorful, boxlike buildings and billboards, scattered leftovers of what feels like a greed invasion that violates the most basic achievements in architectural aesthetics. We are offended, and then we exhale. Sometimes the most offensive things are the only honest things out there, we say, before we look back at the blue dot on our phone, which is, in comparison to the outside, neither beautiful, nor ugly, nor true, nor false—it's just blinking and moving forward in its own virtual no-man's-land.

Fifteen minutes later we leave E65 and turn north-west on Sveta Helena, a narrow country road that cuts through a hilly landscape in green. The rural foreground is animated with small fields of corn and woodpiles in driveways, a tractor and a rosebush. We recognize something familiar about an old metal fence, and a trellis fence in dark wood, and, later, one in white vinyl. We see a barrier made out of concrete elements and some hedges between more houses and grass mowed short, vegetable gardens, and potted plants on fissured concrete platforms. We pick those details like one picks flowers in a meadow. It's comforting to add parts that compliment a cherished idea we carry inside us, the idea of an Eastern European village in a hilly landscape that we've known by heart since childhood. The gooseberry bush, the white house number on a blue enamel plate, and a dried-up fir tree in front of a two-story house are out there to approve who we are, we think; these things are out here to be in agreement with what makes sense to us; these things are that to us now what the walls of our mothers' womb might have been *when we were inside that scenario.* This is what makes it feel implicit, driving through this Eastern European countryside, we say. It feels intimate, yet totally inaccessible at the same time. It's impossible to describe, it's impossible to translate how the ups and downs in the topography relate to who we are—unnecessary, too, because *we are it.* The banalities in the foreground, the hills in the distance—we are deeply embedded, cozily covered with a closeness to something we actually understand, yet only for a split of a second, and then we get thrown out again, the car moves on, the landscape changes, nobody can describe the things one knows best, we say to each other, those things do not exist in words, they never last a syllable, there is no time for them to appear because they are eternal, and there is no space for them to become visible because they are always present, we say as we keep driving by a kind of village villa that has been suffocated to death with a Bavarian-style renovation and then reanimated with red geraniums in flower boxes blooming with no sense of refinement or moderation in those utterly obscene, chemically fertilized, capitalist ways. The only things one can attempt to describe are the things one doesn't know. It only feels appropriate to describe what one can't apprehend, we say, at least it doesn't feel like treason to talk about those brick walls that haven't been plastered and those balconies that have no railings. What is actually up with that? we say. Why does every second building we pass have no wall plastering and no railings on its balconies? Why do the houses look as if they have been left unfinished for decades, bricks and beams, raw and naked, memorials to a not-there-yet-ness *of what?*

"Why?" we will ask the women of the gallery about ten

days later, when we return to Zagreb to drink coffee with them. "No money," they will say. "No money," they will shrug. "No money," they will laugh. "No money," they will giggle. "No money," they will repeat.

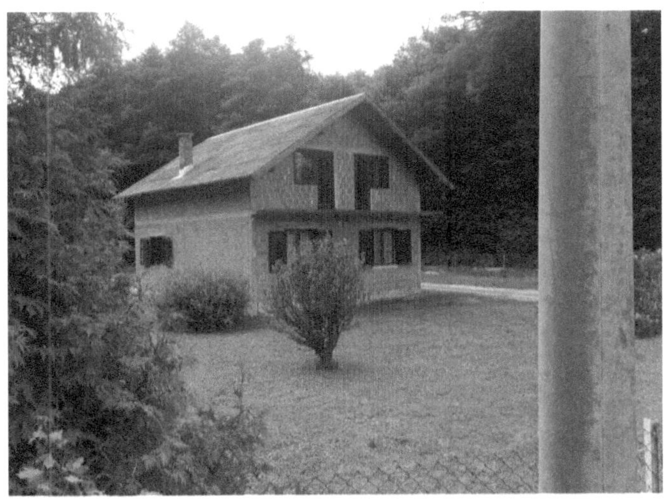

We keep driving. We see on our phone how Sveta Helena eventually turns into Brezovec Zelinski, which then turns into Gradišće, while outside our windows small apple trees alternate with satellite dishes. The next intersection is coming up in eight hundred meters. We switch between the phone and the view outside: at six hundred feet, a weeping willow in a wet spot; at five hundred feet, a heap of wood sloppily covered with a weathered plastic tarp, followed by another house with un-plastered walls; at four hundred feet, an empty lot with a shipping container, dark blue work pants and gray shirts on a laundry line, a heap of sand, a small, narrow ditch right next to the road filled with mud; at three hundred feet, a black SUV in front of a garage that was built for a much smaller car, white plastic garden chairs, a red arrow on a metal sign, then a man with a wheelbarrow; and at two hundred feet, a woman with a plastic bag and plastic gloves, then potted plants that spend the summers outside and the winters on indoor windowsills, and then a black Mercedes right behind us. It's the guys from Kruku, we say, Kruku sent the escort in a W222 Mercedes-Benz S-Class, we say while we try to make out the driver's features in the rear mirror. We turn right on Zagrebačka and keep driving, now switching our attention from the phone to the back mirror to the street, until about five minutes later, when we enter Sveti Ivan Zelina and start looking for Zagrebačka ul. 64. The blue dot on our phone passes by the red pin. The black Mercedes is still behind us. We pull into the next driveway to the right and turn around. The black Mercedes keeps driving on. 68, 66, 62, 60. Where is 64? We turn around, drive back, pass by the red pin again, park at the side of the road, and text the women from the gallery. They text back that they know nothing—only the address— and send us a phone number. We call, let the phone ring ten times, hang up, call again. We turn around again. 50, 52, 56, 58, 60. We drive into another driveway, turn around again, and pull into the parking lot at the #60 Faraon Caffe Bar, which is advertised through a sign on a road that shows the black outlines of an eye with an eyebrow. We get out of the car and greet the sphinx that guards the

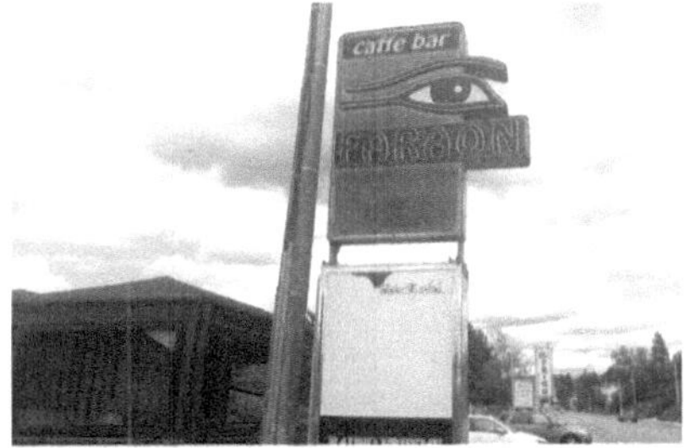

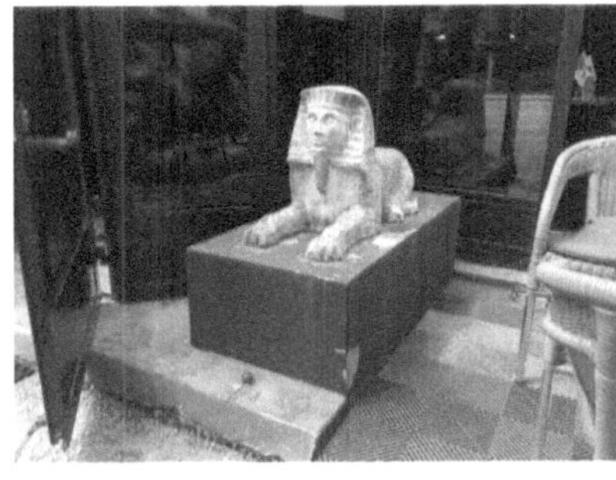

entrance of this former one-family house that has been converted into a coffee bar by adding several glass-enclosed porches, cane chairs, small coffee tables, and ash trays. The sphinx is a *hint*, we think as we enter the first inner room, a space devoid of people, which, despite the comfy leather chairs, round tables, yellowish-painted bricks and an Egyptian wall relief, feels artificially cold. *The sphinx will eat those who can't answer her riddle,* we remember as we now enter a dimly lit, windowless second room, which looks and feels much closer to what we assume it wants to be—an ancient burial chamber that features a giant open sarcophagus in the form of a bar.

The walls are covered with hieroglyphs and Egyptian-style paintings: every head is in profile view. A man sits at a table and drinks coffee, and a woman stands in front of him, both smoking. We clear our throats and smile. Why are we so nervous?

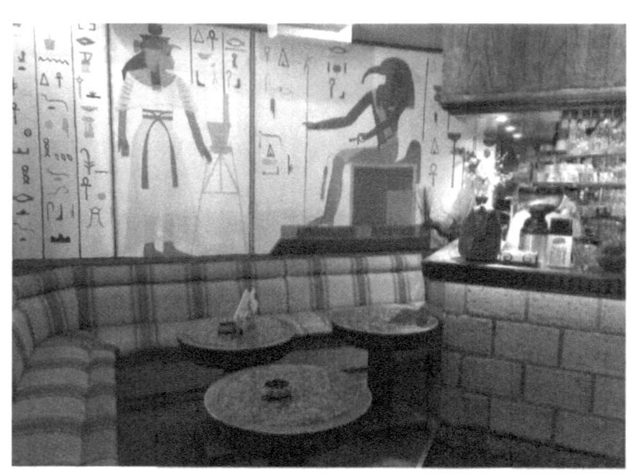

"Kruku" we say. They show no reaction.

"We can't find Kruku. Where is it? Where is Zagrebačka ul. #64?" we say and show the map on our phone to the woman.

"You are #60, right?" No reaction.

"Mislav," we say.

There is a little upward twitch around the right corner of the woman's mouth, which makes us certain that she knows Mislav, but that this doesn't mean she has to tell us. We understand. We would not tell us either for the very same reasons. We ask for the bathroom. She points toward the back of the burial chambers, where the ancient people used to keep their mummification supplies. Since we don't have to pee, we make use of the average toilet time by looking straight ahead into the mirror. What we see looks very uninteresting. We rip pieces of toilet paper and lay it around our heads like bandages, calculate how many rolls of toilet paper we would need in order to reemerge from the bathroom as fully-wrapped mummies, unroll the head bandages, throw them into the toilet bowl, flush, wash our hands, step outside, and look at the wall drawing next to the bathroom that depicts a slim human figure in a white skirt wearing an eagle head or actually with an actual eagle head. A stiffly-seated person, whose elongated head extension looks like a beehive or two abstracted cobs of corn, sits across from the eagle head and offers him or her or it a key and a walking stick. We walk over to the waitress and ask if we can take a picture. The waitress nods. We ask if we can get two coffees. She nods. We keep walking around, looking at the images on the wall, and then sit down in a booth that is decorated with a small standing human figure who offers a flower to a larger seated figure, double in size, and wonder if the smallness of the person to the right in comparison to the large one seated on a stool with animal legs to the left is a matter of physicality, perspective, hierarchy, power, or coincidence. And what is it, actually, that the small person offers?

It looks like a flower, but it could also be a duster, or a brush, or water coming out of a hose. The offering figure has two shoulders but only one fully-developed arm; hence, only one hand. He is missing one of his *grasping appendages,* we say. Is that an ancient metaphor? Or is this just a sloppy hobby painter running out of patience or time to fully render a hand with five fingers on the walls of a coffee bar? It's hard to tell. We keep

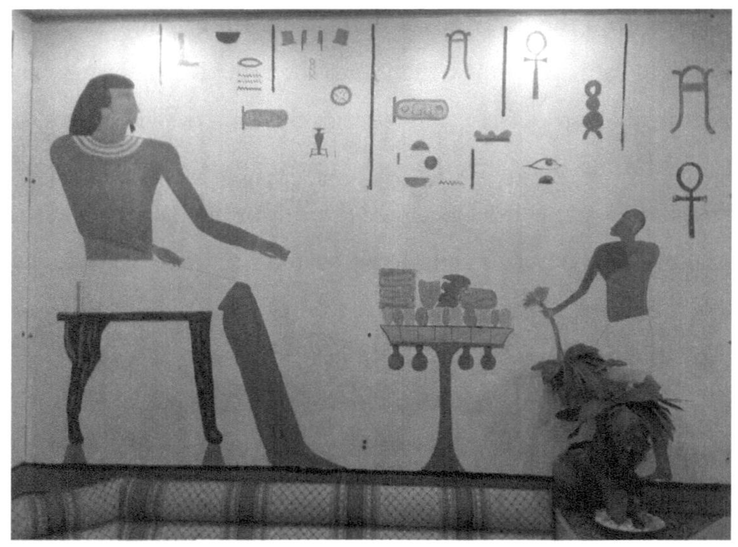

looking. The offering figure is not only missing a hand, there isn't an eye on the side of the face that's turned toward us—yet the figure's chin looks determined. The chin clearly indicates that there is something going on between the small figure and the big one; they obviously communicate with each other. But what about? we wonder. And how?

Between the two figures is a table filled with abstracted shapes—some are stacked on top of the table, some hang down from under the table. Maybe that's how these two figures speak to each other. They pick up an object and hand it over without saying a word, without saying what it could be, without reducing it to *a banana*, or *folded napkins*, or a *piece of cloth*. They physically integrate the object in their conversation without disempowering it by calling it a lettuce leaf, or a piece of bark, or a colony of ants eating an apple core. Isn't it frightening to realize how hard it actually is to see anything without knowing what we are looking at? we say. Isn't it actually wrong to go out into the world and point at a thing and say: It's a table!

We look at the hieroglyphs above the scene for answers. There is a zigzag line and an eye; there is a cross with a balloon on top, which could also be a magnifying glass with a sword handle, or a faceless stick figure in a long dress that sings songs in a choir. There is something braided. It could be hair, or straw, we say, or is it dough? Or is it a bundle of joy in a crib making its mother the happiest and most fulfilled human on earth?

The waitress brings the coffee. We thank her, add some sugar to the coffee, and stir slowly. It's impossible to picture what Wittgenstein meant when he wrote *that the hieroglyphic writing pictures what it means.* We have never read more than a few random quotes by Wittgenstein, yet as we think about that one quote from the internet our intuition insists that *he must have known.* Otherwise he could not have said it so *simply,* we reason. That's the crazy thing about intuition, we say. Nothing is closer to the truth and further away from the facts.

We call Kruku again. Nobody picks up. We open a web browser and search for a hieroglyph translator. There are many. The braid is supposed to be an h, the zigzag stands for an n, the magnifying glass is nh. We are excited, but then the mix and match game gets boring. It feels wrong to have all the unknowns reduced to one or two letters of the alphabet. We close down the hieroglyph translator, type in *Ancient Egypt*, and read about ancient deities, and then about the afterlife. We read about hymns and prayers, we read about the funerary texts, we read about powerful people—the lords of the two lands, the rulers of Upper and Lower Egypt, the pharaohs who made the laws and collected the taxes and defended Egypt against foreigners. We keep scrolling down the timeline of the ancient universe as it keeps revealing itself to us on our phones, we keep sipping coffee and keep clicking on links, yet nothing really speaks to us—it's all just data that does not register, the words don't have power, there is no magic spell in the way they are written out. We scroll and scroll until we come across a photo of an actual amulet that depicts, we suddenly realize, the almost exact shape of the narrow eye that is featured on the road sign outside. Recognizing the amulet as being the original source of the road sign feels like a major discovery, and like a cat who can't be stopped to show his or her owner the dead bird she has caught, we now can't be stopped from jumping up and presenting the waitress our booty—the amulet on our phone—full screen:

"The Eye of Horus," we say to her with beating hearts. For the first time, her stern expression softens, but that's all. We return to the table and sit down. The sphinx is not yet satisfied, we say.

There is a house. One enters it blind and comes out seeing. What is it?

We keep reading.

There is a house. One enters it blind and comes out seeing. What is it?

We keep reading.

There is a house. One enters it blind and comes out seeing. What is it?

There has never been a riddle that has not challenged us, yet finding the answer always made us feel uneasy. There is always something very uncomfortable about attempting to find an answer. On some level, searching for the answer feels like killing the riddle, we say, hence, the closer we get, the more we slow down. We sit here and sip coffee. It's very typical, we say. Once a year, we go on a so-called research trip to a country we have never been to before, and what do we do once we get there after months of planning? We sit in a coffee bar and scroll through the internet, drink coffee, and say: *The curse of every riddle is its answer, yet without an answer, there would be no riddle. That's the actual riddle.*

We order two more coffees and keep going, keep reading about the cosmos and then about *heka,* a linked word, linked to something like magic that shouldn't be understood as something mysterious or extraordinary. Heka, it says on the internet, was an everyday tool for the people who lived around the lower Nile around five thousand years ago. Heka, it says, is a force; heka is the capacity to make things happen by unintentional means; heka, the Egyptians thought was a natural phenomenon often applied for religious rituals, yet regular humans could use it for personal purposes as well. We smile: that's all we need to know for today. We put some money on the tray and wave the waitress goodbye.

It's bright outside. It takes a while for our eyes to adjust. We stand in the parking lot and look into the clouds. The clouds are puffy. There are puffy clouds in the sky, we say, and recall why we actually came here, which then makes us realize with some surprise that Kruku has lost its power as being the most important thing to do today. Things have changed. It's only been an hour and a half, and she did it again, we say, checking the time on our cell phone. The world has moved on. We stand there calmly and think about the fact that having read about Ancient Egypt and about heka on our handheld device in the burial chambers of the Faraon Caffe Bar in Sveti Ivan Zelina—a town with sixteen thousand inhabitants, twenty-seven kilometers northeast of Zagreb—feels equal to having visited Kruku. We stand there and wonder how it actually happened that wanting to know more about *heka* has almost replaced wanting to visit *Kruku*, why it feels as if the ten letters that make up the word *Egyptology* have overridden, one by one, the ten letters that make up the word *camouflage*, we say, as if by sipping coffee in the burial chambers of the Faraon Caffe Bar, the motivation to understand how the civilization of ancient Egypt eventually came to an end is as genuine as the urge to understand the techniques used to make objects, animals, or soldiers invisible in contemporary warfare. We don't know what to do about this realization. We are confused. We lack ambition, we say. Since we had written our unsuccessful funding proposal to the Croatian Ministry of Culture about needing two thousand dollars in order to fly from NYC to Zagreb, rent a car, study the relationship between camouflage and concealment—between naturally blending in and actively hiding—by visiting Kruku's production facility, we had consistently talked about Kruku. Kruku had been the main objective of our research trip, Kruku had been the reason to fly to Croatia, yet now—two house numbers away from the place we had claimed was so essential to our investigations, we read about heka and call it a day?

Everything happens for a reason, our neighbor used to say. We get into the car and type the address for the next stop on our travel route, Kneževi Vinogradi, into our phone. The estimated travel time is three hours and forty-five minutes. We put the gear in reverse and start backing up, but are stopped by the man from the burial chamber, who, during the last hour had not exchanged a look with us even once. He spreads both arms away from his big body and slowly walks in front of the back of the car, then turns around. The tip of his fingers demand that we follow him. His left arm straightens, his fingers tighten, he rotates his arm, and then all his muscles relax for a second before they tighten up again with even more urgency, which tells us that there is basically no way out of this anymore. Heka, we say as we drive through an open metal gate down the private road behind the coffee bar rather reluctantly. To the left are some trash bins, to the right is a two-story brick building that could be, judging from several spools of thread that sit in one of the windowsills, a textile factory. The road makes a right turn in order to wrap around the backside of the building, yet our attention is drawn to the left toward five brown plastic flower boxes that are standing in a piece of grass between a small elec-

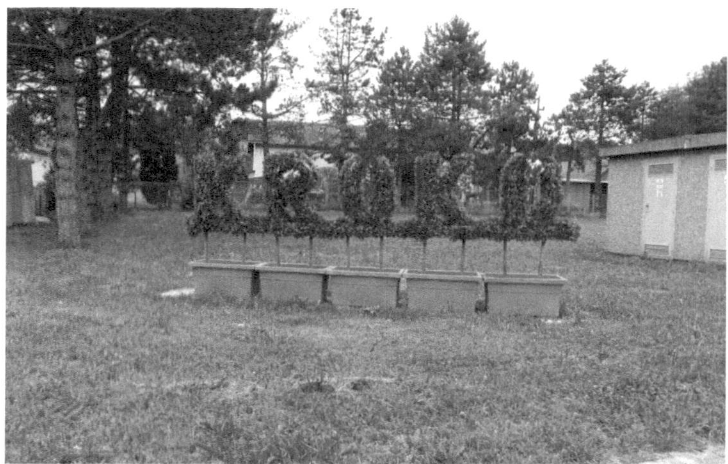

trical building on one side and some metal dumpsters on the other, all in a line.

Each planter holds up two sticks, which hold up a three-dimensional letter seamlessly covered with small dark green plastic leaves. It's hard to actually see the green-covered letters against the green grass in the background. We have arrived.

The main entrance is an unassuming back door. We press the white button and a woman's voice asks us a question in what we assume is Croatian.

"We are eteam and would like to see Mislav," we say.

After about three minutes, the door opens. Mislav, a friendly man, shakes our hands, apologizes for his English, and then leads us through a hollow-sounding, narrow corridor that leads to a set of stairs, which leads to another hollow-sounding corridor and then into a big dim room on the second floor with

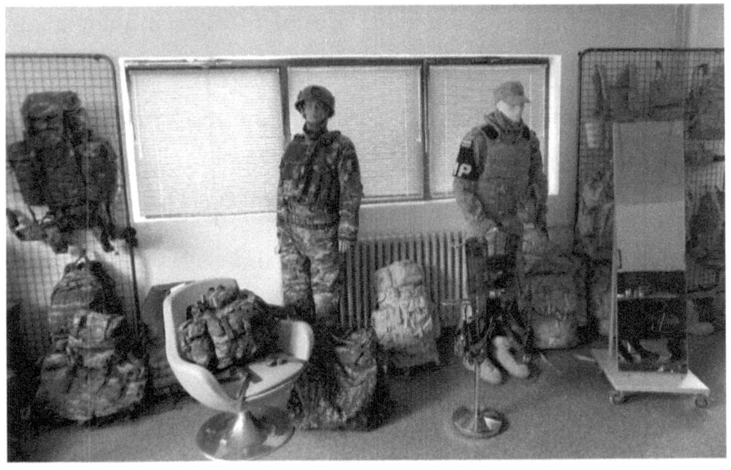

a low ceiling. Mislav apologizes for the cluttered room and points at four half-empty coffee cups that sit on a big brown table among several camo textile swatches and a notepad. He says he will get someone to clean up the mess, which makes us predict that he will now go out and call a woman, which turns out to be true. An elderly woman with gray hair enters the room and takes away the coffee cups. As she shuffles out the door, Mislav makes an awkward gesture to sit down in the office chairs surrounding the big table. He asks us what we want, and we say that we want to know how it happened that the shape of Croatia, the outline of Croatia's appearance on a map, became part of the Croatian battle dress. He says he doesn't understand. He gets up again and says that he needs to get a translator. We ask if we should wait here. He says yes and leaves the room. We get up and walk around the outer parameter of the room, which is lined with several life-size human mannequins, each wearing different parts of camouflaged combat uniforms, helmets, hats, vests, pants, ammunition belts, and hip bags with all kinds of pockets, leg halters, and boots. Backpacks, travel bags, and several automated machine guns are propped around their feet and against the walls, and each soldier comes with his own color scheme—some are dressed in a mix of blue, some are beige, some are dark green, some light green shades. We picture Croatian soldiers canoeing through the ocean and crawling through a jungle and walking through the desert and hiding in a woodland.

Mislav reenters with a young woman. We sit down again at the table. The woman asks us what we want. We say that we are wondering about the outline of Croatia being part of the Croatian camouflage uniform. Who came up with this idea and why? She translates our question to Mislav. He shrugs; she smiles back at him. We follow their lead, shrug, and smile back at them. Mislav asks if we want coffee. We say yes. He looks at the young woman. Coffee? he says. She says yes. He gets up and leaves the room again. The woman starts laughing.

"Why are you laughing?" we ask. "Oh, it's nothing," she says. And then she laughs again. And then she says, more to herself: "That the boss gets up and gets me a cup of coffee . . ."

"What's your name," we ask.

"Magdalena," she says, and then we tell her our names. She gets out her phone and looks at her screen. Mislav comes back with a tray and three cups of coffee on saucers. The coffee smells like filtered coffee that ran through a machine that doesn't heat the water hot enough. We know we won't be able to drink it, and we already feel bad about it because Magdalena had been right, it must have been the first time in Mislav's life serving coffee on a tray. Each coffee cup spills a bit over the saucers as Mislav puts them down on the table with a slightly shaking hand. Magdalena bites her lip.

"Can we take some pictures of the mannequins?" we ask.

She translates. Mislav looks exhausted. He says something to Magdalena and she translates back to us that he has to ask the boss. He gets up again and leaves the room for the third time.

When, about ten minutes later, Zvonimir enters, his presence spreads like wildfire. Naturally, we jump up and extend our hands.

"Women first!" he says cheerfully, brushes the man aside, and encapsulates the woman's right hand in his warm, powerful grip, just long enough to make sure we understand the rules. We understand, sit down, cross our legs, and smile.

"So you know my brother?" he says.

"Your brother? No," we say.

"How did you get here then?" he asks.

"You put the address on your website," we say and mentally salute the women from the gallery who had called Mislav persistently, again and again and again over the last month, until they finally persuaded him in their charming ways that eteam visiting Kruku was an excellent idea.

"And what brings you here?" Zvonimir asks less cheerfully. We suddenly blank. We have no answer. We try to think, but nothing comes to mind as we stare at Zvonimir's fingers drumming on the table, nothing but a quote:

"All warfare is based on deception, Sun Tzu said in *The Art of War*," we say. Zvonimir stops the drumming and lets the quote linger in the air right in front of him for a while. He takes his right hand and gives it a little push. When it comes down again, he pushes it up with the palm of his left hand, juggles it back and forth a few times, and then leans back and smiles. The quote hovers twelve inches above the table. He has set the baseline. We nod.

"Go on," he says.

"Did you read the book?"

"Go on."

"You are in the business of camouflage. What exactly does that mean?"

"I manufacture products that make it hard to detect soldiers and their equipment in combat."

"Are you aiming for invisibility?"

"Possibly," he says with a hint of a smile.

"How can you sell a product if the advantage of your product over other people's products working in the camouflage business would be its total invisibility?"

Zvonimir frowns.

"If you are to be truly successful," we say "which you could be, technically speaking . . . if you produce a combat uniform that renders the soldiers invisible in their environment . . . not only would nobody want to buy that invisible product, nobody would go to war anymore either."

"Why?"

"Because nobody wants to die *unseen*."

"Sun Tzu said that?"

"No."

"Who said it?"

"Soldiers, wearing tiger stripes."

"Go on."

"To be a successful businessman, you can only produce uniforms that have built-in faults. You can only produce failures, the failure being the paradox that the human in the uniform must still be visible, otherwise not only would it become impossible to recruit soldiers, there would also be zero motivation for the enemy to kill. Who wants to go out there and kill a man who is not there?"

"It's a tough job," Zvonimir says.

"Yes, and you've got it figured out."

"Yes, me and my brother."

"How many people do you employ?"

"Around three hundred, and we keep expanding. It's all happening right below us. If you are quiet for a moment, you hear the sewing machines, ratttatatat, ratttatatat, ratttatatat, ratttatatat," he says with a tiny touch of hostility.

"Would you show us the production facilities?"

"No."

"How come?"

"It's a secret operation," he says with a serious look on his face.

"Why do you have so many uniforms on display here?"

"You said yourself, these uniforms are *failures*. I am not a pretender. I don't like to deceive people. Like you, first thing, I put my shortcomings on display."

"Why?"

"Same reason you put on an apron for cooking."

"We don't put aprons on for cooking."

"You like to make yourself vulnerable?"

We bend our upper bodies ever so slightly forward, as if the blob that just blobbed out of the pumpkin soup we are cooking in our kitchen landed slightly above our navels on an unprotected white T-shirt. He seems very pleased with the reenactment.

"Why do you have so many different kind of uniforms on display?" we say as we straighten up again.

"We've been recognized beyond Croatia for our exceptional quality. We sell our products and services to the Germans, to Switzerland, to Kuwait, Saudi Arabia, Montenegro, Kosovo, South Africa. Every country has their soldiers employed in different climates and terrains, and we've customized our designs to their specific needs."

"You produce for whoever comes along?"

"I produce for whoever pays me. You got any money?"

He knows how to input certain variables in order to get certain outputs and keep the situation in control. We are jealous of this skill. Zvonimir smiles, gets up, and waves us over to the Saudi Arabian mannequin, where he shows us the heavy thread he uses to sew his garments and talks about the tailored cuts of his outfits.

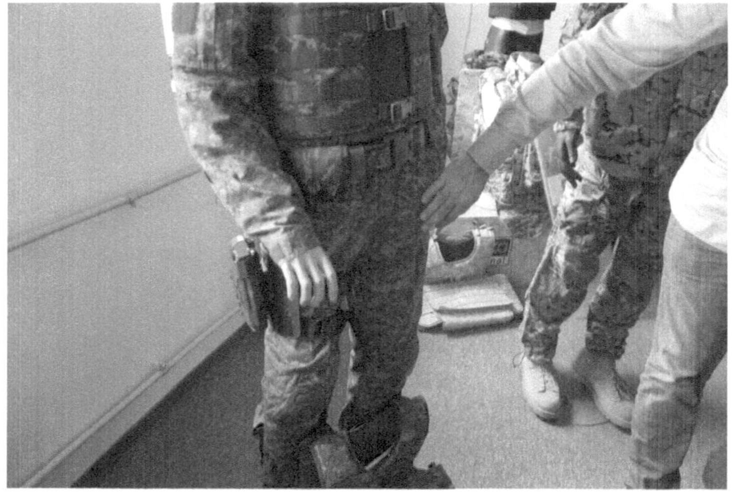

"It's imperative to have a cool cut," he says. "It increases confidence and morale. Why do you think women gravitate toward men in uniform?" he asks.

"Women like being around humans fighting for the survival of their babies," we say.

"You got it," Zvonimir says. "People who can't provide a sense of security by showing off their money have to put on uniforms. It makes it easier, you know . . . to cocreate. The American military calls it the "CDI factor," the chicks-dig-it factor. You guys should go to the library and ask if they have a book on that."

"What is it called again?"

"The CDI factor."

"Do you have a piece of paper and a pen?"

"You want to write it down? Let Magdalena write it down for you. Magdalena, write down: CDI factor. That is spelled C as in camouflage, D as in deception and, I as in Idiots."

Ordering Magdalena to write down stupid notes for us is the territory beyond which we won't advance. We look at his forehead and spell it out— calmly and sincerely—one eyelash at a time: m o t h e r f u c k e r

Zvonimir gets it; he is highly trained.

"Which uniform do you like best?" he asks and makes an open, inviting gesture with his right arm to reconsider and look at all his products that line the perimeters of his show-room.

We get up and try to concentrate, try to ask more questions about camouflage, but suddenly we can't, can't concentrate, drift off instead of looking at the mannequins, wonder how it would look—in retrospect — later in life —— later in history ——— to slowly walk eight steps backward, bend our knees, pick up the machine gun that leans against the wall with our right hand, walk over to the trash bin, stuff it in, exit the build-ing, and eat an ice cream.

It would look good, we think, kind of revolutionary even,

we think. Yet, as we go over the plan again, a second time, we realize that it has a major flaw: *the trash bin doesn't look like a trash bin*. The trash bin looks like an expensive design object. One can't stuff a machine gun 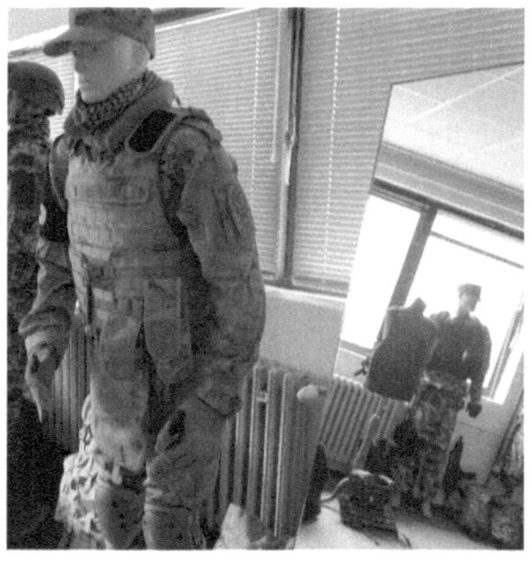 into a trash bin that looks like a piece of art, we think. If we were to make a point in stuffing the machine gun anywhere, it would have to be a flimsy wastebasket, a beaten-up aluminum bin or a shitty cardboard waste basket or a stinky trash bin, and not a sturdy, proudly shining oval-shaped metal container that is seamlessly covered with a fake wood texture that comes pretty close to looking like precious mahogany. Zvonimir beams with pride about his trash bin. We lost. He won. He clears his throat:

"You want to know why I integrated the map of Croatia into the camo uniforms?" he asks.

We shrug our shoulders.

"War can be very confusing," he says. "It can get foggy out there. Ever heard about the Fog of War?"

"Is that a mental thing or an actual smoke bomb that gets

exploded to hide something?" we say.

"It's both. Anyway, having the shape of the country a soldier fights for as part of his uniform helps to avoid misidentifying comrades as the enemies. It minimizes the casualties from friendly fire,—if you use infrared, the shape is even more apparent."

"That is the reason? How many soldiers die in friendly fire? Two percent? Five percent?" we say.

"It's not about the material aspect. It does not matter how many. *One* is enough to derail an entire mission, an entire army. When troops who expect to be targeted by the enemy are being attacked by their own forces, their morale goes down rapidly. They will start doubting everything—the meaning of war, the competence of their commanders—and that in turn will make the commanders more cautious in the field and less likely to win. Technology guarantees us a high level of precision, but that precision is always in competition with those human certainties and uncertainties. War is a very human endeavor, certainty is linked to confidence, and once the certainties begin to erode, the chances of winning decrease dramatically."

"So the shape of the country is something to rely on when in doubt, a symbol of allegiances? This cluster of brown pixels is a reminder—in case the soldier forgot why he was killing people?"

"Yes, because war is no place for having doubts. People like you would be the first ones to die, most likely in friendly fire,“ says Zvonimir and smiles a smile so genuine, it almost makes us think that he has built his whole military production facility to defend highly endangered people like us.

“Would the three hundred people below us mind if we keep you busy a moment longer and tell you a story?” we ask.

“I am the boss. Let’s sit down again,” he says.

We sit down and lower our heads.

“When we were about nine or ten years old,” we say, “we had this idea that if we could render the *perfect* outline of a white dove, world peace would be *unavoidable*. It all depended on *the perfect outline*, we kept telling ourselves. This was most likely driven, as you must know, by the incomprehensibilities of the cold war terrors in the Eastern Bloc. If the shape of the dove was perfect, we thought, people looking at the dove would realize that bombs and wars were not the solution. The dove, we thought, could have this power to convince people to believe in peace—the dove just had to be precisely the shape that could contain the idea of peace with such overwhelming logic that it would make it irresistible  to think and consequently act otherwise. The dove would not only have to symbolize peace, it would have to be peace itself.”

We look up from the table. Magdalena looks bored. Mislav

looks sleepy. Zvonimir's eyes are pointed directly at ours. They are blue and see-through.

We worked on the dove, and once we thought we had gotten pretty close to the perfect shape, we transferred the cardboard stencil to white paper, cut out the dove, and brought it to school where we pinned it with a needle through the eye onto the so-called classroom wall newspaper, a cardboard piece covered with thick red felt, a political tool to disseminate political propaganda in the form of cutout newspaper images, headlines and hand-drawn slogans.

Not one person paid attention, not even our teacher, Mr. Meisner. We went back home, made the beak a little smaller and the wings a little bigger, cut a new stencil, and then cut out thirty paper doves, which we pinned the next day all over the much bigger wall newspaper in the school's hallway, which was not cardboard covered with felt, but rather a wood panel covered with felt, a detail we hoped would add a lot of *weight* to the pinned-on messages. Yet again, nobody paid attention. This time it seemed purposefully out of good will—basically to save us the embarrassment of having to comment on our utterly naive attachment to world peace. We stood in the hallway after the bell rang, frozen inside with anger and disappointment, when a boy came out of the bathroom. He stepped close to the wall newspaper and looked at the cut-out paper doves long enough and with enough sincerity to make us assume that he understood everything and that he shared our conviction, that he also thought that the symbol of the dove was powerful enough to spread world peace."

We pause. Magdalena scrolls through her phone. Mislav has closed his eyes. Zvonimir looks absentmindedly in our direction.

"Remember the hallway?" we say. "Remember the days when it was socially acceptable to think peace had a chance?"

"Maybe," Zvonimir says slowly. He turns his head and stares out the window. We join his stare.

"You think I was that boy?" he says after a while, still looking out the window. "Let's pretend I was that boy. Let's pretend I looked at the doves. What did I see? You want to know?"

We nod.

"I saw the perfect shapes of one hundred doves, yet all were blind. Instead of an eye, they all had a needle head that pinned them to an ideology."

He is right, of course. We never thought about that.

"So?" we say.

"Great ideas that work so hard not to see are stupid."

"Yes, and . . ." we say, hoping he will teach us something important now.

"Did it stop me from falling in love with you?" Zvonimir says calmly, still looking out the window.

"No it didn't," he answers to himself. "Let's say it's true. I fell in love with you."

"OK," we say.

"Naturally, you never loved me back," he says.

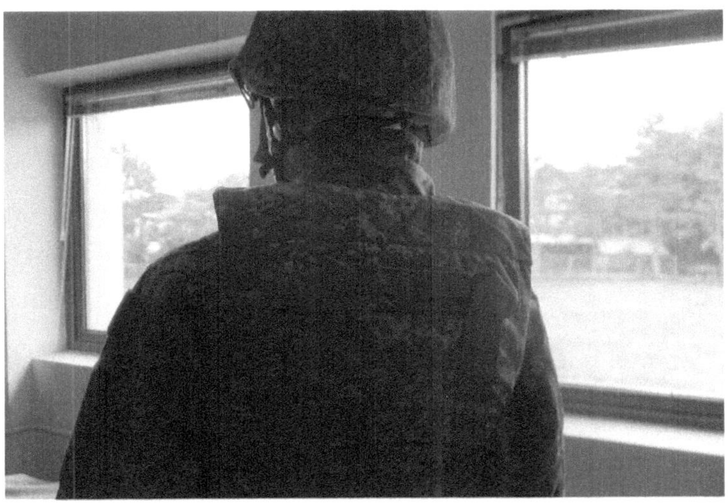

To a GPS system, every destination is a red pin, and all coordinates are equal, a set of numbers that specify a location on earth. The further we drive north, the flatter the land and the bigger the fields become. We see fewer and fewer cars, and then suddenly, the highway *ends*. There is a booth with an absent-looking attendant that marks this end, and after that, there is an abstruse loop that may have been installed to facilitate a sort of transition into pre-or-post-territory by providing two hundred meters of asphalt. And then there are sunflowers. Millions of sunflowers, tall and straight and stiff, all pointing their heads in the same direction. It's strange, what this does to one's sense of being in the world, we say as we keep driving through the partitions of an enormous field, each part separated by a narrow canal filled with water. Sunflowers, we had read on our phone in Zagreb, are, next to corn, the most arable crop in Croatia. Sunflowers. Sunflowers. Sunflowers. Heavy-headed summer bloomers, the apprentices of the sun, day in and day out they track the center of the solar system from east to west, and at night, they turn back east to face the rising sun in the morning once again. Yet once they mature, they settle down and only face east, we say, which makes us suddenly picture how concentration camp inmate Simon Wiesenthal, on his way to clean medical waste at a converted army hospital for dying German soldiers, comes to a halt on a crossroads in the countryside. To the left of the road on which he stands with a group of fellow inmates, he spots a military cemetery. A sunflower is planted on each grave, which fills Simon Wiesenthal with envy of the dead soldiers as he imagines that through the sunflowers, those dead soldiers are still being connected with the living world, while his future dead body, he knows, will not have that connection, as it will end up in a mass grave, where, instead of flowers, dead bodies will be piled on top of him. Once the group arrives at the hospital, he is taken to the bedside of a twenty-one-year-old dying member of the SS, who feels the urge to confess to a Jew the war crimes he has committed against Jews in order to ask for forgiveness from a Jew and obtain absolution. Wiesenthal listens to the stories in horror and leaves the room in silence, only to wonder later if he had done the right thing. Should he have forgiven him? Could he have forgiven him? We shudder. *This* question, surrounded by an army of industrialized, meticulously aligned, sun-obedient sunflowers takes on such monstrous dimensions, our bodies act primal, chose flight over fight and push our thoughts to a time when the systematic extermination of six Million people within a four-year time span had not occurred yet. Van Gogh's decapitated withered sunflower heads lay peacefully on a table. Did you know that van Gogh painted the withered ones before he painted the blooming ones in the vase? we say. Yellow ray florets, a yellow vase, a yellow background, yellow on yellow, cadmium, lemon, ochre, orange, pollen, pale, and bright.

"Merde!" Gauguin had said when he saw the painting.

"Everything is yellow!" he had said. "I don't know what painting is anymore!" And when he followed Vincent's invitation and came to Arles, the house was painted yellow, and the rooms were painted yellow, and on the yellow walls of the rooms hung paintings of sunflowers and Vincent was glowing in the sun, and Gauguin, his mentor, was painting *Vincent painting sunflowers,* which became the only painting Gauguin actually completed during his two-month stay in Arles in 1888. *Van Gogh Painting Sunflowers,* we say. Naturally they got into fights, and the idea that van Gogh cut off his ear as a result of his quarrels with Gauguin went unchallenged until two art historians suggested that Gauguin chopped off the ear with his sword in a fight. The actual proof of the theory is not that the art historians dug up van Gogh's ear to investigate what kind of blade separated it from Vincent's head, but a comprehensible rewriting of the story, which lays out that it is as likely that Gauguin chopped off Vincent's ear as Vincent doing it himself. Nobody will ever know, we say, and most likely they wanted it this way, because they kept *a pact of silence* about the incident, which makes one wonder in which ways sunflowers are directly connected to *silence,* we say, driving through the field. They simply don't talk. They don't nod their heads. Sunflowers don't even smell, we say. They don't care that, after some of their ancestors were eternalized with so much intense inner feeling by one of the most radical and influential painters in the history of Western art, Vincent eventually shoots himself in the chest with a revolver in a *wheat field*, they are simply not moved by the fact that thirty hours after the bullet was stuck in his chest, Vincent's last words to Theo were:

"The sadness will last forever."

The only thing that moves them is the sun, and *this* is where it sits, we say, *the forever lasting sadness* he talked about. It sits right here between the mercilessness of the sun and the endlessness of these monocultured, gene-manipulated, pesticide-powdered, chemically fertilized fields, we say, when the road makes a left turn in an exact ninety-degree angle and the next field starts, this time occupied by multibillion-dollar (or Croatian kuna) repetitions of green, multicellular organisms called toxic corn.

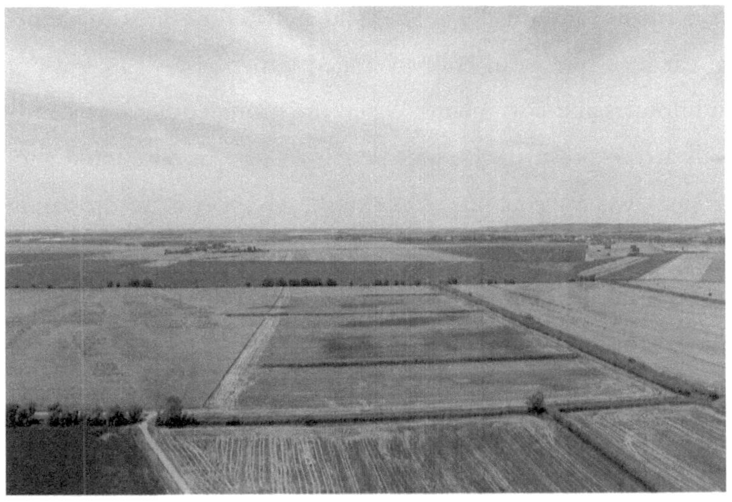

We drive through the field in the manner of a first-person-shooter video gamer moving through a maze—we keep driving mildly alert and numb at the same time, until the next intersection forces us again to turn our vehicle in a precise ninety-degree angle, this time to the right. We turn and keep driving through corn, until we reach the next intersection, where we have to make a ninety-degree left turn again. We stop the car, park on the side of the road, take the black casket out of the trunk, and screw the four small propellers onto the body of the drone. We turn on the handheld screen, and then hold down the power button until the drone's propellers spin fast enough to mimic scifi insects. We grab the little joystick and let the robot rise up into the air, and as it goes up, we see ourselves on the screen in our hands being dwarfed, we see ourselves getting smaller and smaller as we stand, in real time, next to a rental car in a European country called Croatia between rows of sunflowers and corn plants. When the drone comes to a standstill at the pre-programmed height of one hundred and fifty meters, we wave at ourselves. Look, we say, we are drowning in an ocean. We jump up into the air and it feels as if a snowflake lands near the Northpole. We walk a circle and it makes us think of a cow wagging its tail. We throw a rock and picture how the wind just picked up and carried away a particle of dirt in a desert like Rub' al Khali, one thousand kilometers long and five hundred kilometers wide, nothing but sand. We do a jumping jack and realize, with that frightening sense of certainty, how a blue bacillus divides itself symmetrically to make two daughter cells. *Irrelevant*, we say. Completely *irrelevant*—us being on earth. Absolutely pointless. This self-inclusive God's-eye perspective simply blows up our ability to be *on* earth, to be a grounded human. It's brutal, we say, pointing at the screen in our hands, and what's brutal is not the aerial view—we have looked out of airplane windows at the world below us without being disturbed—what's so frightening is the stillness of the gaze that includes ourselves from a height of one hundred and fifty meters in real time. The camera does not move; the distance is too great to detect the sunflowers moving their leaves in the breeze, it's too far away to notice that we are talking or breathing. There is no movement on the image. Everything is *still*. Still as in life-less, still as in *still-life*. The drone sits like an unmovable rock at a height of one hundred and fifty meters, unperturbed by winds, unimpressed by birds, unfazed by the stillborn creatures its camera eye faces on the ground. We are rendering a dead world, *we are deadly*, it's us right there on that distant plane, we say, and point to the tablet in our hands. It's us appearing in our own hands on this alienated rectangular patch of virtual earth. Maybe the military can handle such a point of view, we say, but as civilians we should get out of here, we say, and start walking with the handheld screen and the remote control toward the field, where we enter a random row. There is enough space between the stalks and the leaves of the sunflowers to walk through. The ground is dry, there are cracks in the dirt, it's a little cooler in there, the heads of the sunflowers are right above our heads, the big green leaves have a scratchy surface, they scratch the skin on our hands and arms slightly as we shuffle them to the side. Their leaves are like sandpaper, we say, and wonder if the field would be big enough to grind us down if we kept walking from beginning to end of every row through this field . . .

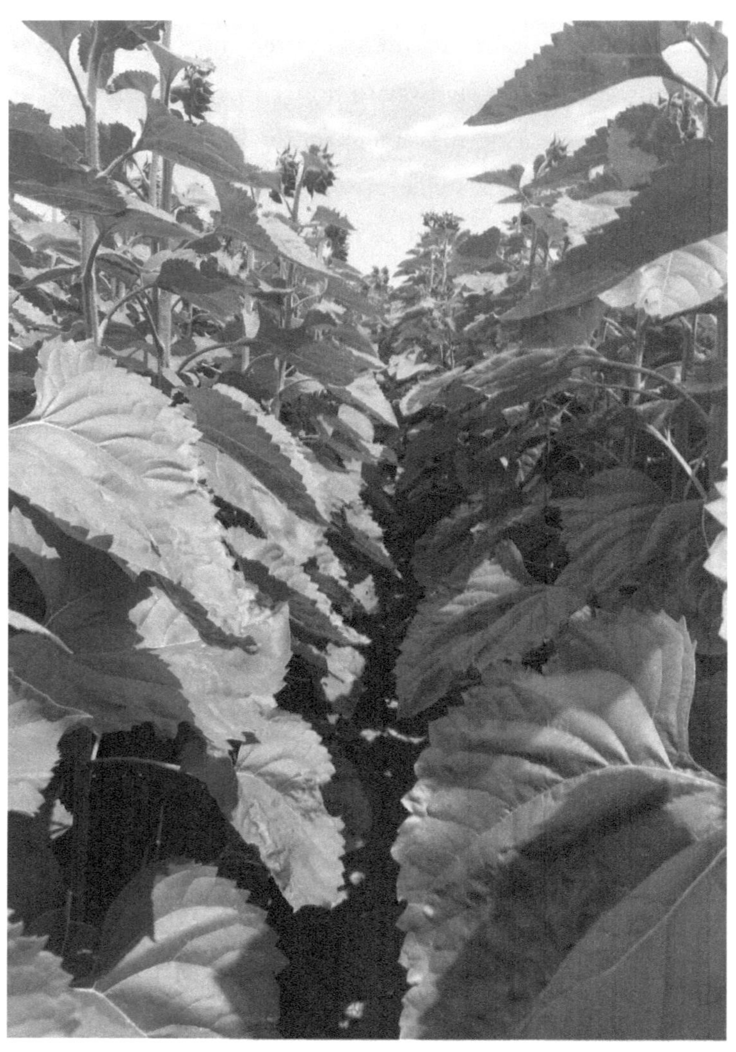

Row by row,

we sing,

into the tunnel,

worn away by friction,

ground into fiction.

Step by step, we sing,

out of sight,

into the field,

like a knight.

Row by row,

into the field,

if we keep going,

we might be healed.

Step by step,

into the field,

revealed and concealed.

The one who sings is the one who stumbles ahead slightly out of rhythm, the other one follows silently, balancing the tablet and operating the drone above us.

Row by row,
into the tunnel,
abraded by friction,
ground into fiction.

Step by step.
out of sight,
into the field,
like a knight.

Row by row,
into the field,
revealed is the bitter
concealed is the better.
Does it really matter?

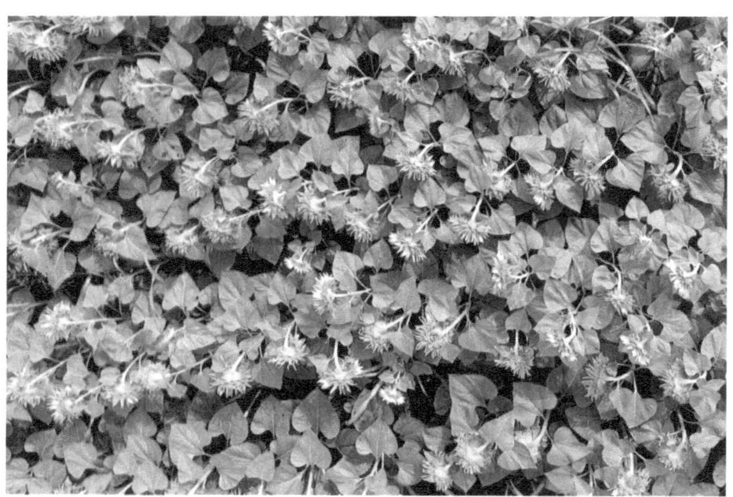

Eventually we stop. We look up and through the green leaves and the yellow petals into the blue sky. The light is bright; we squint our eyes. We search, yet we can't see the drone. The drone must be there, hovering above us, we hear it in the distance—or at least we seem to hear it, yet we can't see it. We look down again at the handheld device on our screen—there are only green rows of sunflowers. We are *gone*. We have walked far enough for the road and the car to be out of the camera's periphery; we have walked deep enough into the field to witness in real time our own disappearance.

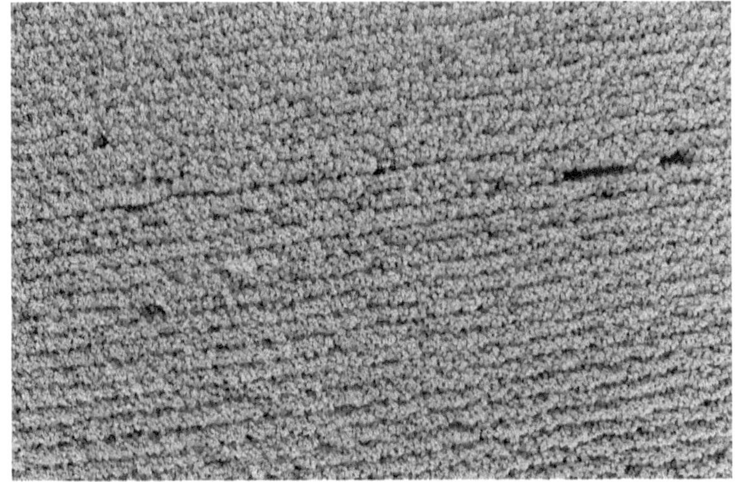

Four hours later we enter Kneževi Vinogradi, Osijek Baranja County on Glavna ulica. It is 5:34 p.m. on August 5, 2016. Kneževi Vinogradi seems to be another pearl in the string of road villages we have been passing through for the last half hour, and, like the others before it, the settlement seems to consist mostly of one long through road in the middle, alongside which, shooting off in ninety-degree angles, lay towel-shaped properties, all similar in width and length, on a flat surface. If one treated the middle road as a spine and folded this village along the white centerline of the road, it would roughly match on both sides. There would be a general symmetry—a strip of mowed public grass followed by a public sidewalk, then a private fence, a narrow front yard with private flowers, then somebody's private house, then a garage or a barn or a shed, then a vegetable garden, then some grass with fruit trees and a couple of private berry bushes, then another fence with a smaller gate, then a public dirt path, then a small field, then a bigger field or fields on persistently spreading flatness. Every property in a road village has roughly the same layout and therefore the same outlook, we say, hence, when the road villagers look out of their living room windows across the street, they most likely see properties and lives that mirror their own. This mirror effect comes with certain advantages and certain disadvantages. Most people respond to this situation by lowering their blinds to a certain degree at certain times of the day; most people actually respond by having their blinds shut down all the time. From the outside, one might think the amount of rolled-down blinds are in accordance with thermodynamic temperature regulations, or in response to the weather, while in reality they are an act of mental health regulation, we say as we keep driving down Glavna ulica, now paying attention only to the *closedness* of the blinds. Some are down halfway, some are down three quarters, some are down one tenth, some are down one sixteenth, some are down one twentieth or even one thirtieth. These kinds of positions require highly trained roll-downers, we say. To leave such a tiny slit open requires not only skill, but also a very specific intent. The people in Kneževi Vinogradi are certainly among the most specialized and refined people in terms of lowering win-

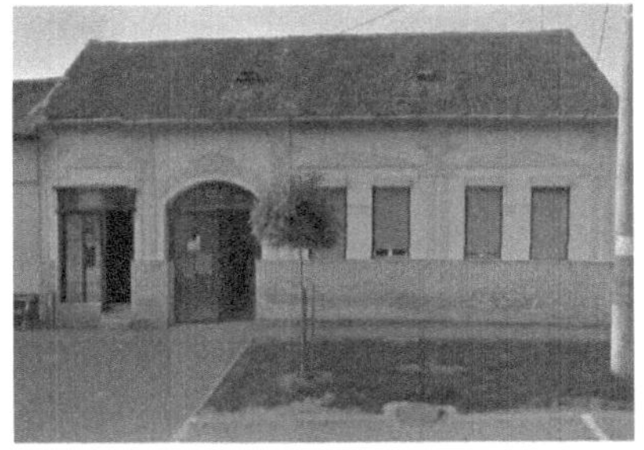

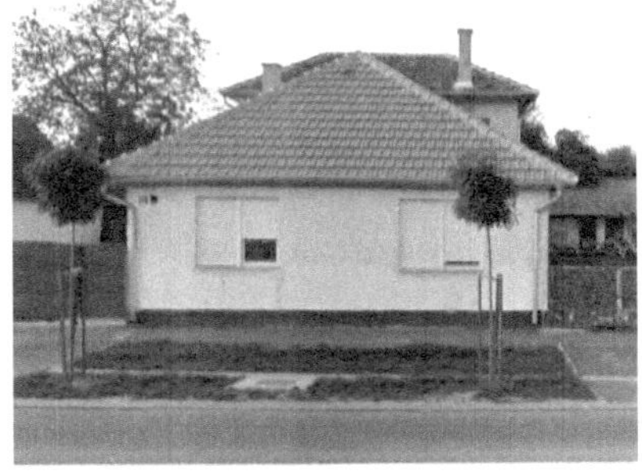

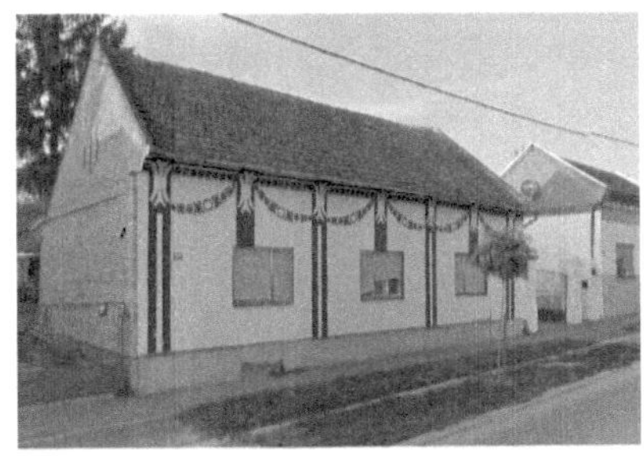

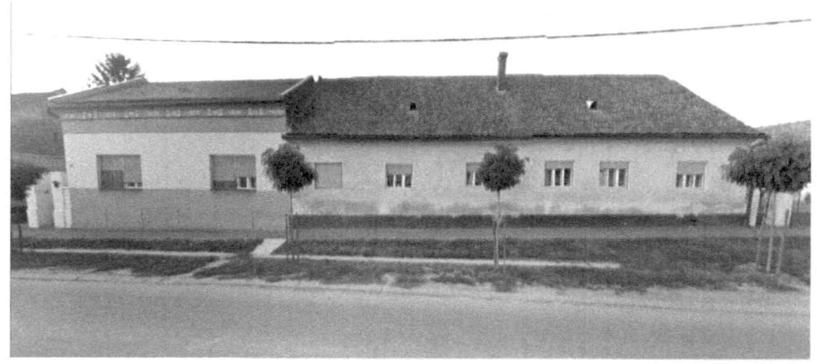

dow blinds. One always thinks that German people show the most dedication to precision, but that is just a myth, we say. The German blind roll-downers simply look like a bunch of rough guessers in comparison to the people of Kneževi Vinogradi.

Glavna ulica, we say, now looking straight out the front window again at the road, is what enables the road village and kills the road villager. That's the dilemma with *through roads*. They don't even pretend to be anything else but a way to get away, which is demoralizing if one has a place called home so closely connected to a situation like this. It must be very unsettling to have one's place in life attached to the constant dominance of this *through-roadedness,* we say, and to have the passage of time and goods and people and cars constantly exemplified in front of one's door with such brutality. Road villagers, we say, can't allow themselves to think *along* the road—they can't even attempt to imagine what comes further along the road, or what came earlier, they always have to think *across* the road. In order to survive as road villagers, one can't do anything else but resist the road, constantly resist the inescapable *throughness* of the road, which naturally leads to this perpendicular attitude to life that makes the typical road villagers not only the least traveled people, but also leads to their straight up, inflexible, always resisting, upright attitude through which one can tell a typical road villager in flat lands apart from a scattered villager in the mountains, for example. The phenomena of the road village is very motivating, we say. One can drive through a road village and think about *the road-spine*, and then drive through the next one and think about *the perpendicular attitude to life*, and then drive through the next one and think about *the blinds.* One can spend a whole tank of gas driving through foreign road villages building up a heap of guilt for doing nothing

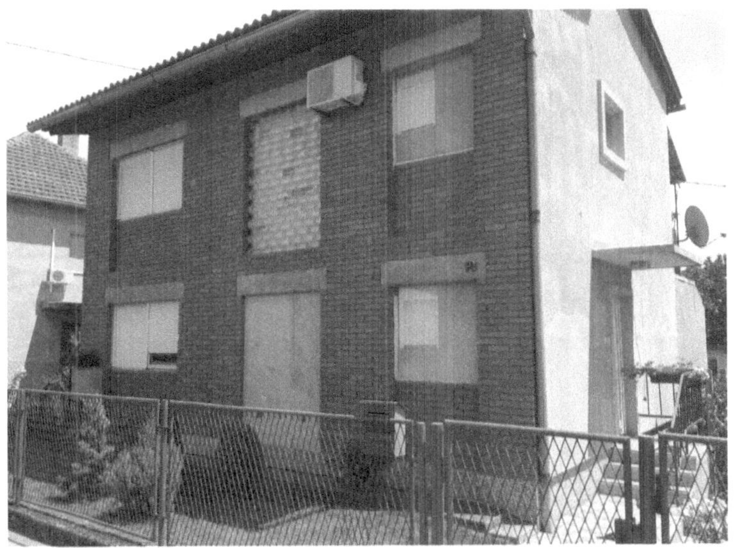

but driving through them and treating them in the most stereotypical manner, as foreign road villages that consist of not much more but utilitarian free standing houses and stables and barns, some a few hundred years old and some only a couple of decades old, all more or less the same practical boxes with two or three or four small windows, a door, and a shingled roof. Eventually, though, we say while turning our heads again to the side, one realizes that sprinkled in, here and there, between the most basic facades of the most utilitarian houses that haven't been repaired or painted for many decades, one starts to see some details that fall outside the category *most basic and utilitarian*. There are houses out there, that have decorative frames painted around their rectangular windows, like this one over there, we say, and point to a freshly painted facade where garlands come down from the gutters in formal bows. These are the hammocks in which the good old times swing back and forth, we say, back and forth being the motion we associate with being cradled in the certainty of recurrence. Some houses have circular windows in their gables, some have wrought iron gates made of hearts, others consist of volutes and dainty flowers through whose hollow spaces the one-night-only-serfs-turned-princesses of age-old fairy tales are escaping their homes in horse carriages when they attend feudal events in monastic interiors. Maybe it's those specific colors that trigger such thoughts, we say. Maybe it's the feudal, faded pink

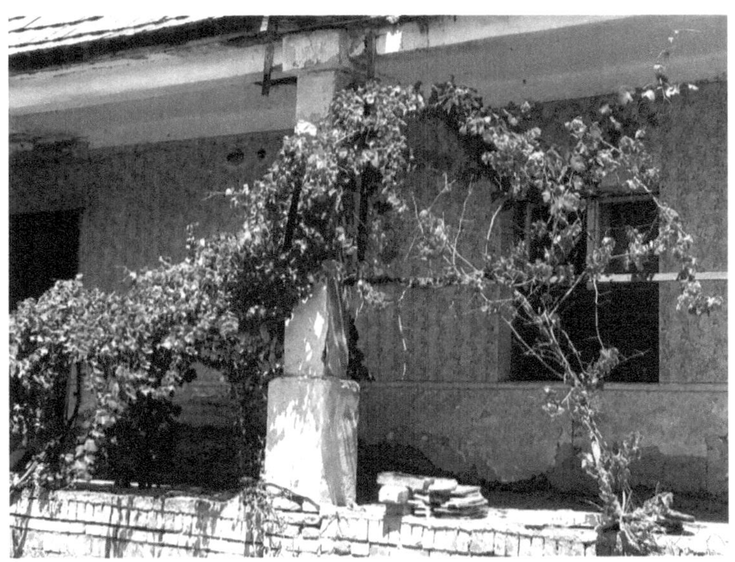

or that noble turquoise paint peeling off that door over there. Maybe it's the Slavic stencil work in chestnut brown on white, the sturdy shapes of floral ornaments with which the walls of that built-in porch are covered. Maybe it's the way some ornaments are rolling and spiraling horizontally along the house facades in incomplete circle motifs of vines and flowers, as if they are opposing the gravitational forces of vertically growing trees and plants. Maybe we are simply looking for something nice and comforting, we say, while also looking for #156, the number of our accommodation. Maybe it's us procrastinating and deviating, maybe we should do what this village actually *demands,* and drive *through* the whole village first, we say, before we resist the *throughness* and stop at our accommodation. Maybe we are doing it all wrong. Maybe we should drive back to Zagreb and spend the night there and then come back here in the morning and look for #156. Maybe it's easier to approach #156 first thing in the morning, instead of at the end of this day when we are tired and whiny, we say at the moment the red pin and the blue dot of the digital map in our hands start to merge. We stop the car on the side of the road. There is no number on the house, it's gray and small, all blinds are closed. We walk to the gate; there is no bell but a big, dead rat in the driveway. This can't be it, we say, and if it is, we can't stay here tonight, we say. If this is truly #156, we have to call the women from the gallery and tell them that #156 is not acceptable, we say as we get back into the car. Further down the road is a woman walking toward us on the sidewalk. She is the first human we've seen on the sidewalk of Kneževi Vinogradi. We get out of the car again and walk toward her. She wears pajama pants and pink fluffy slippers. We show her the address on our phone and then point at the house with the dead rat our car is still parked in front of and shake our heads and cross our arms in a capital X. We say NO, and show her the address on our phone again. NO, we say and repeat the X with our arms until she does the same. She points at the house and shakes her head and says NO, and since we don't speak each other's languages, we keep pointing and shaking, saying NO, NO, NO, until the pointing at the house and shaking of our heads releases a piece of collective burden that makes us feel a little lighter. We smile and then the woman smiles and then we all laugh and then the laughing is over and we get back to our car and the woman keeps shuffling down the sidewalk in her pink slippers.

People in these kinds of road villages have two pairs of shoes, we say as we turn around in order to drive down Glavna ulica in the opposite direction. They have the street shoes for the front and the rubber boots for the back. When they leave their houses through the front, they put on their street shoes, and when they go out into the fields through the back, they put on their rubber boots, and that makes all the difference. In the end, it's simply a minuscule detail that decides everything. It's some random fact that makes us who we are; it's the footwear that decides if people become front or back people, if we become trained in deciphering the world by looking at house facades, raked gravel patches, windowsill decorations, curtains, blinds, and shutters, or if we become conditioned to understand life based on the layout of vegetable gardens, size of cucumbers, lengths of dog leashes, number of heaps of raw building materials, and rabbits in cages, and draw our conclusions from the way the back of a house bleeds into nature, or how so-called nature transitions into the so-called man-made world, or the public into the private sphere, we say while driving down the main road of Kneževi Vinogradi, when we suddenly arrive in front of #156. It's a small detached house with red geraniums, big enough for a small family and allowedly much more inviting looking than the house with the rat in the driveway. Yet we don't feel able to enter the dwelling and temporarily join Lena's family, Lena being the woman who according to the women from the gallery lives in there and rents a vacation apartment in her house. We get back into the car and start eating a chocolate bar. It's no surprise really, we say, that the women from the gallery have booked the most affordable accommodation after the entire funding from the Croatian government fell through, and maybe it's all for the better, we say, to be as close to this basic kind of Croatian life as possible, since this is not a holiday but a research trip. We finish the chocolate bar, get out of the car, and ring the bell, and five minutes later, we sit with Lena and her second husband Vilmos in the back of her house at a wooden table, drink schnapps,

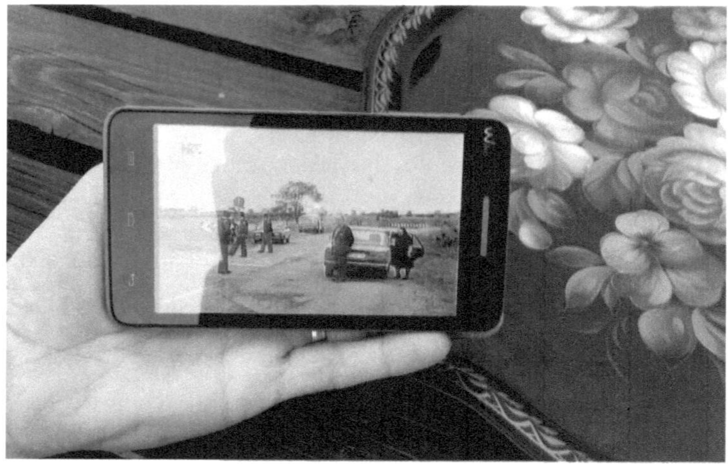

and look at the phone in Lena's hand on which she replays a three-minute documentary video about the Serbian soldiers invading Kneževi Vinogradi to this day twenty-five years ago.

"You came on the day of the twenty-fifth anniversary," she says while we look at tanks rolling down Glavna ulica, the road we had driven down not even ten minutes earlier. Lena speaks German and she likes Germans. She feels indebted to Germans, because it was the country of Germany that accepted her and her two children after they fled through Hungary. She spent seven years in Germany cleaning a small German hotel in Peissenberg. It was a good job, she says, because the hotel was newly built, "no old dirt to scrub off," and her boss was a good man. He put a little table and two stools in the ironing chamber so her sons could do their homework while she was ironing the bed sheets, and when her sons got in trouble in school, her boss came with her and talked to the principal. She has good memories, even though the room they stayed in was just a regular hotel room and did not have a kitchen. But they managed—she got a hot plate and put a curtain in the middle, and her sons got the side with the window and she got the other side, and both of her sons stayed in Germany after she returned to Croatia, they stayed in a German boarding school—it was better than coming back to this mess. She visits them twice a year. She has two grandchildren now; they all speak German, none of them Croatian.

"Life takes sudden turns," she says. She left her house and her life from one day to the next in 1991. She was lucky to be able to escape, because she spoke Hungarian and told the soldiers she was going to Budapest—and that's what she did, she went to Budapest first. She knew she had to leave when she heard her neighbor's son had disappeared and her friend's husband hadn't come home. That's when she knew it was time to go. She paid a friend of her mother's and he drove them the next day, her and her two boys—she was divorced at the time. She left with a suitcase, and she came back seven years later with the same suitcase and a new husband. They cleaned up the house. It was badly trashed and half destroyed, but Vilmos worked very hard on it and renovated it nicely. We should feel very comfortable in this house, Lena says, and shouldn't be concerned about the neighbors, who are Serbian, she says. It's a Serbian family that built this new house right over there three years ago, yet they never bothered her. It's all back to normal now, all back to regular living, she says, then pauses and adds:

"So you came here to go to Liberland?"

We are startled. Since visiting Liberland means crossing the Croatian border into unknown territory, we are not prepared to talk about this idea with two strangers we have just met.

"How do you know?" we say.

"I asked the woman who booked the apartment on the phone: Why do two people from New York City want to stay in my house?" Lena raises her eyebrows.

We nod. From the moment we saw her, we liked her. There was something wholly womanly about her, something motherly, feminine, fierce, intelligent, and caring—one could tell from her big breasts and her mouth and in her brown eyes that are covered with a cloudy film. We wonder how old she might be. Sixty-five, seventy, seventy-five?

"How did you hear about that Liberland?" Lena asks.

"We found it on the internet," we say.

"What does it say about it on the internet?" she asks and puts her elbow on the table and her thumb under her chin and her index finger on her cheek. This is not some polite backyard chitchat. Lena wants to know.

"As far as we can tell," we say, "Liberland is a self-proclaimed micronation that claims a parcel of disputed land on the western bank of the Danube river, not so far from here. It was occupied last year, in April of 2015, by a Czech man after he had realized that due to a border dispute between Croatia and Serbia, a piece of land, about seven square kilometers in size, was actually unclaimed territory. He got a flag and a pole and stuck it into the mud, and defined the borders of Liberland so as not to interfere with Croatia or Serbia.

"This is the floodplains. They constantly change, they flood, they dry up, they appear, they disappear," Lena says. "Our government wants the borders the way the Danube meandered before it was streamlined, and the Serbians want the border the way it goes now. The governments can't agree which border is the right one. It's been going on for years."

"Swampland," Vilmos says. "It's all just swamp area. It's like a maze of small islands and rivers. The Danube has formed an inner delta around here—you can't really build anything there. There are many rare birds there though. People go to see the birds, but there are even more mosquitoes. Billions of mosquitoes. They will eat you alive."

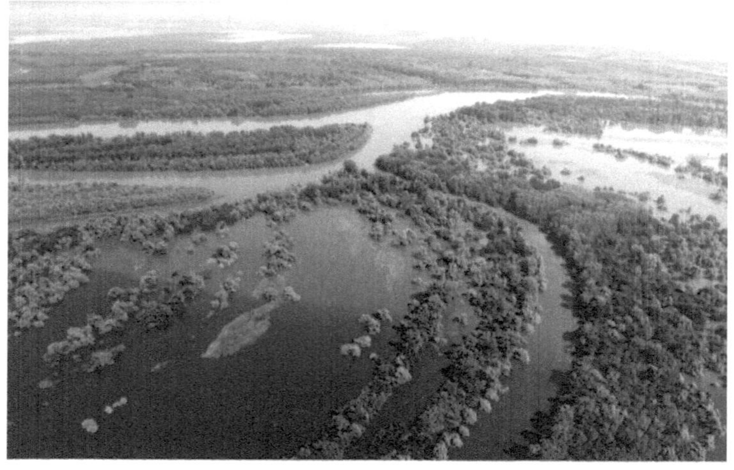

"I read about it in the newspaper. They got the Czech man arrested, " Lena says.

"Yes, we read that online, too," we say. "Croatian police got him arrested several times, but they can't prosecute him because he entered the area from Serbia, and as long as Croatia insists that this territory constitutes part of Serbia, he has done nothing illegal. They have to let him go. He has discovered a loophole around a terra nullius and he uses it openly. He has published a constitution, he has set up a website, he has a bank account where you can donate money, and so far four hundred thousand people have applied for citizenship. Four hundred thousand people have filled out the forms to become citizens of Liberland," we say.

"What kind of people?" Vilmos asks.

"People from the US, people from Russia; six thousand people applied for citizenship from Syria," we say. "Liberland's motto is: To live and let live. It's kind of libertarian. No taxes, free market economy—they envision the state to be run like a corporation runs a city. They are deeply skeptical about the idea of a welfare state like Germany. They like America as a model. They point out that the German constitution is one hundred and forty pages long and written in a language nobody can understand, while the American constitution is only twenty pages long and very simple, which is actually kind of amazing, if you think about it."

"How long is Liberland's constitution?"

"Thirty-five pages. The man who wrote it, a young student, said he needed the extra fifteen pages to spell out more ways through which citizens can legally get rid of the government, if the government starts getting corrupt and stops serving the people."

"So they are a group?"

"The main force is the president, the Czech man who put the flag in the ground and claimed the territory, but he has attracted many others. They are quite active. They issue video statements on the internet, they have recruited voluntary diplomats in other countries, they hold conferences where 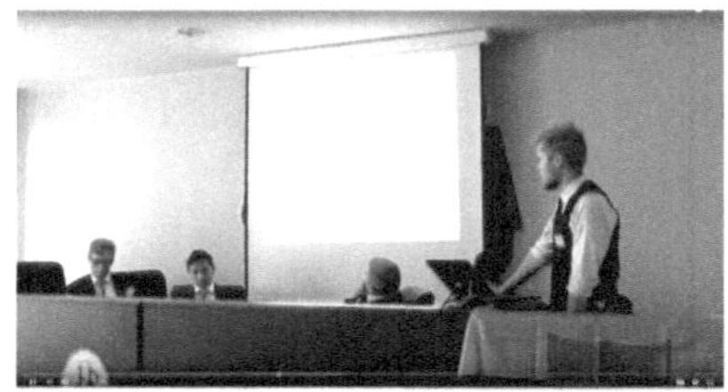 presenters show up in black suits and red ties and give Power-Point presentations that explain their ideas about the creation of a new state in the middle of Europe. They take it very seriously. It's a hands-on experiment in politics that is based on the real grounds of a no-man's-land."

"And you want to join them?"

"No."

"Why not?"

"Thirty-five pages is too short for a constitution," we say.

"How many pages would suit your state?" Lena asks.

"Three thousand," we say. "Or five thousand."

Lena smiles. "Do not simplify that which is complicated."

"Exactly," we say. "What's the law of the land, if the law only talks about the people and their legal requirements but not about the land, the soil, the trees, the microbes, the earth-worms, the butterflies, the rocks, the stars, and the birds? There are supposedly two hundred and sixty different species of birds in the area of Liberland, hence, one would already need at least two hundred and sixty pages to account for these birds. What's the law of the land if it doesn't take into consideration the forty species of fish that live in the inner delta region of the Danube? Why talk about liberty, freedom, supreme law, taxes, and making a distinction between legal and natural persons without talking about the tree those people will smoke their electric cigarettes under, without talking about pike, ide, bream, carp, catfish, and pike perch, and how they fit in a can and how that can fits on a shelf in a supermarket? What makes us curious right now is actually not what the people will do to the land, but rather what the land will do to humans who are willing to listen. What sort of obligation is the white water lily going to establish in the branches of Liberland's administration? How does the forceful taming of the formerly wild Danube in the nineteenth century inform the establishment of a Free Republic? Is it possible to enact freedom in the middle of a tamed river?

"So you need to go there?"

"Yes."

"I looked it up before you came. I said to Vilmos, let me look where that Liberland actually is, just to make sure. Coming from Croatia you might need a canoe. We got pressure from the European Union. They sealed the border last month because of the refugees crossing the border illegally. I imagine you are going to run into the police, so bring your passports, I would say. Now. First you have to drive to Lug. When you get out of my driveway you take a left on Glavna ulica and then on the roundabout you take the third exit. It's Zagorska ulica that takes you all the way to Lug. That will take you twenty minutes. In Lug there is one intersection. If you were going straight, you would go to Osijek, and if you turn left you come to Kopacevo Tikves. You turn left right there, and then you have to keep driving to Zlatna Greda. They built an ecology center there. You can eat lunch there. The food is good. They have schnitzel with buttered potatoes. If I were you I would eat the schnitzel. There are people there who know the area—they might be able to help you. You might need to hire a guide," Lena says, and then she shows us our apartment, which must have formerly been the food pantry adjacent to the kitchen. Vilmos expanded it, though, he added a space for a shower, a toilet, and a sink that is so small, we can lay our toothbrushes across its edges. There is no window in the apartment, and no door between the bed and the bathroom, but there are two outer doors, one permanently locked and covered with green cushions that presumably leads to Lena's kitchen, the other one a glass sliding door that lets in light and opens into the small backyard. There is a bunk bed on one side of the main room and a double bed. We lay down in the double bed around 10:00

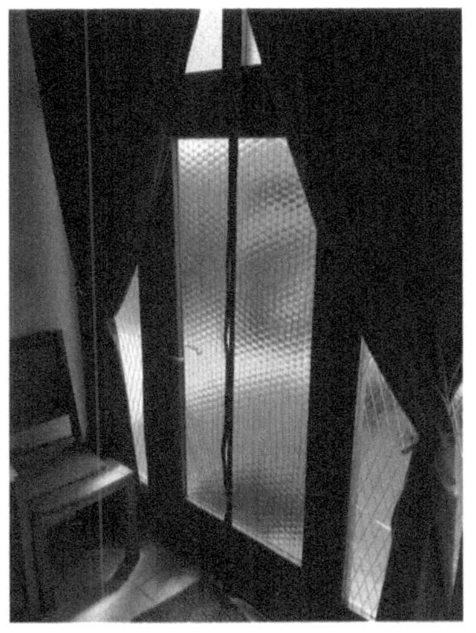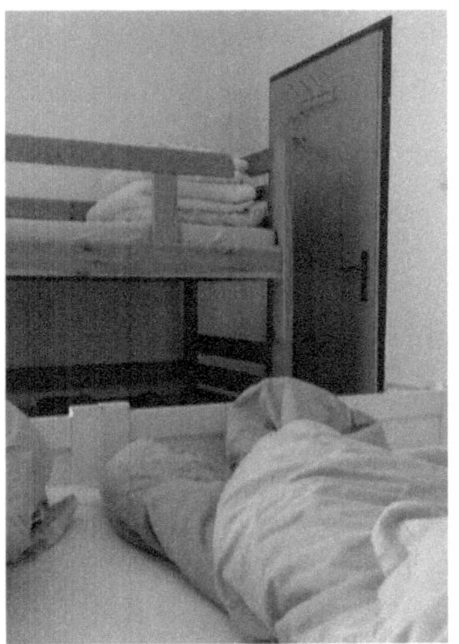

p.m., turn off the light, and listen to Lena rummaging around in the kitchen next to us. She cleans dishes. A spoon or a knife or a fork drops into the sink. She opens a cabinet and puts something in. Maybe a cup or a can, maybe even a plate; it could be either, but if we had to testify in court, we would say it sounded like a cup. She closes the cabinet and then she opens the trash bin, which, according to the squeaking sound, could be a metal bin with a foot pedal, and takes out the trash bag. There is silence for a while and then we hear her relining the trash bin with a plastic bag that must be a former shopping bag. Relining a trash bin with a shopping bag sounds completely different than relining a trash bin with a trash bag that comes from a roll one bought in a supermarket, we whisper while Lena lets the lid of the trash bin drop with a bang. Shortly after the bang, there is a knock on the glass of the sliding door.

"Are you asleep already?" Lena asks through the door. We get up and open the door. She stands in the dark with a small flashlight.

"I forgot, but I need your passports," she says. "It's the law. I am going to bring them back tomorrow morning."

We are hesitant.

"It's the law," she says. "I need to take down the names and addresses of people who are staying in my house."

We don't feel like handing over our passports.

"Could you come in and write down the information here?" we ask.

She comes in and sits down at the small table that serves as a nightstand and a breakfast table and stares at our stack of camouflage outfits and the equipment that is charging and blinking on the first and second row of the bunk bed: a drone, two video cameras, two external hard drives, two digital photo cameras, two cell phones, two laptops, an iPad and a GoPro Camera, all connected to multiple power strips that plug into the two outlets in the room and distribute the electricity evenly.

"I also brought you this mosquito killer," she says and gives us a big red spray can. We give her a piece of paper from our note-pad and a pen. We shiver. It's cold and we are only wearing underwear and a T-shirt.

"Go back to bed," she says, and so we crawl back under the

warm blanket and watch her as she sits right next to us with the flashlight and copies our data onto the piece of paper.

We leave the next morning. We talk to the guide at the ecology center who tells us that Liberland is flooded right now.

"It is inaccessible," he says. "The land is submerged. It's not there."

We drive toward the swamps until we reach a dam that separates the land into dry and wet, into lush and depleted, into wild and civilized. There is growth and chaos on one side and barren rigidity on the other.

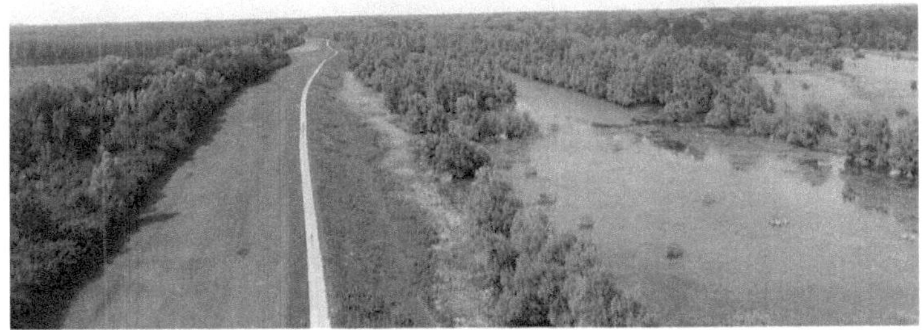

We send the drone toward the swamp. We let it hover over the surface of the water and try to follow a herd of wild boars. We use a lot of mosquito spray. We keep driving along dirt paths through the wetlands. Sprinkled in between tall grasses and bushes are abandoned houses without glass in their windows, overgrown with vines. And then, here and there, houses that still function, houses that still house people who wash their clothes and hang them on laundry lines behind their houses, houses that house people who own cars they park near the entrance gate. What is this area? we say. Is this a nature park, or a biosphere reserve? Is this an extended border strip? Is this the zone where people went missing and where the refugees are crossing over into now? We keep driving. On a sort of mead-

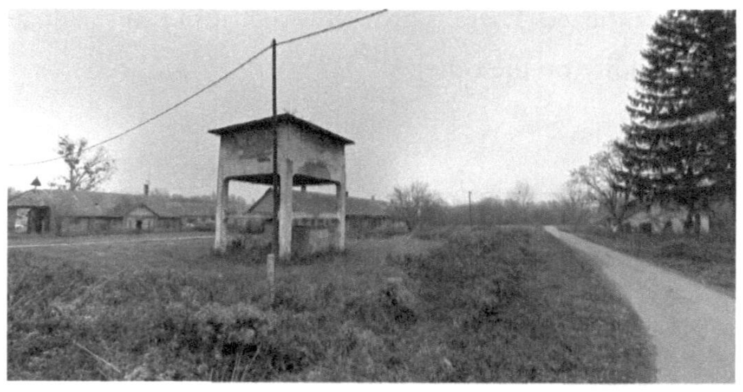

ow stands a watchtower made out of concrete. There are no stairs going up to the watch room anymore. The windows and the door are closed off with bricks. We keep driving on a narrow road through a lush forest of green trees and picture people with backpacks and people with suitcases running through the woods like hunted animals. We think of Lena's neighbor's husband who went missing twenty-five years ago. He went missing around here. Someone shot him and let him rot, we say. There is a dark, human rottenness in these swamps, we say as we pass by a thick, natural fence, grown out of thorny bushes, that separates the wetlands from a field that must have just been mowed down. It's legal to drive on these roads, we say. We are tourists, we say. Bird watchers. We are ornithologists specializing in phylogeography, the study of the historical processes that are responsible for the contemporary geographic distributions of dead and living people. Underneath a tall tree stands a police car. We pass by without looking at the border guards. Why are our hearts beating so badly? Why?

We drive back to Lena's house and then back to the swamps, and test the Kruku camouflage shirts against different back-

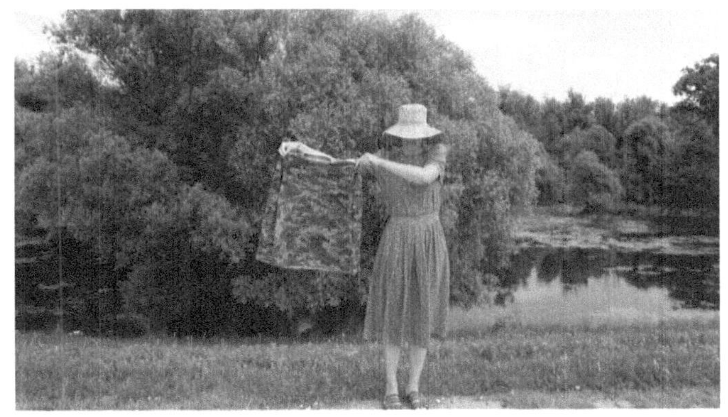

grounds. We cross the border into Serbia via an official check-point and show our passports and order fish soup that a man is cooking in a pot that dangles over an open fire right next to the Danube. There is a domesticated female pig walking around, followed by eight piglets. The mother does all the sniffing and

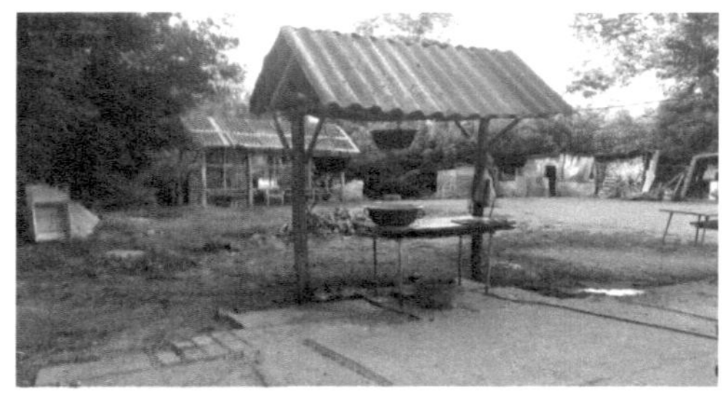

grunting, while the piglets jump around and play. After an hour, the soup arrives in a pot covered in sod. The carp in it tastes like a one-hundred-year-old creature who has gotten incredibly fat from eating decaying river mud his entire life. Feeling guilty, we throw his meat under the table, where three cats are licking his matter off the concrete platform we are sitting on.

We are getting nervous, when the officer at the border asks us why we want to enter the European Union.

"What is the purpose for entering the European Union?"

"The beach" we say, "we want to go to the coast."

Back in the former pantry of Lena's house we read about the police shootings in Dallas. On July 7, 2016, Micah Xavier Johnson ambushed and fired upon a group of police officers in Dallas, killing five officers and injuring nine others during a Black Lives Matter protest, then fled inside a building, where police killed him with a bomb that was attached to a remote control bomb disposal robot. It was the first time U.S. law enforcement used a flying robot to kill a suspect. We keep reading the reactions on social media. "Someone got shot on my timeline—what can I do about it?" a woman asks. It's ten in the morning. We draw a blanket over our heads and keep our eyes open. At eleven we put on our bathing suits and drive toward the Danube. We park on a dirt road in a forest, walk into the river, and start swimming. Our intention is to cross the border in the middle, but when the current becomes too strong we turn around. Lena brings us flowers we can eat; they are branches she broke off a red currant bush and put into a vase. She brings us coffee. She brings us cookies from the supermarket. We drive into the wetlands again, put on a different set of camouflage outfits and hide behind a tree. We notice that many trees in the wetlands are

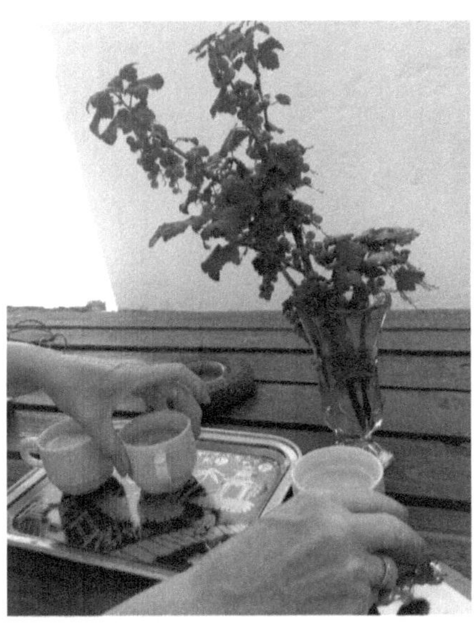

penetrated by mistletoes, parasitic plants that are able to survive by tapping the stems or roots of other plants to obtain water and minerals. We get out of the car, look up, and greet the mistletoes in the crowns of big ash and elm trees. It's the substance of the mistletoes that one of our mothers keeps injecting via syringes into her body instead of doing chemotherapy in order to suppress her cancer. It has been working for five years. Thank you parasites, we say to the mistletoes.

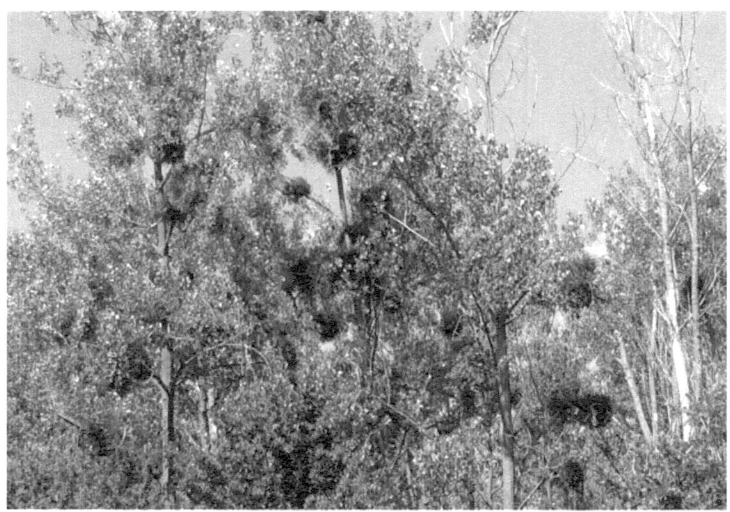

We send the drone up again, and again, and again. Everywhere we go, we send the drone up into the air, and every time we look at the footage we feel further detached and frightened. Lena insists that we go with her to the public pool. We go with her.

The pool is one giant rectangular metal bathtub, surrounded by cornfields. We fall in love with the pool and want to stay in Kneževi Vinogradi forever. Every morning, we say, we will walk down Glavna ulica and go to the bakery. We will buy some cheese-filled pastries and then we will go to the coffee bar. We will sit down in the coffee bar and drink coffee and eat our cheese pastries. And on the way back to Lena's house, we'll stop at the supermarket, buy some bottled water, and then go to the public pool and learn some Croatian. We will sit at the public pool with Lena and watch the people in front of the cornfields and learn five new Croatian words each day, and then we will go back to Lena's house and work until late at night, doing our so-called art work.

We text the women from the gallery that we need more time in Kneževi Vinogradi. One more day, we write, and then the next day we text again and say we need another day. The women from the gallery insist that we drive to the coast. It's too beautiful to miss, they text. It sounds like a tourist trap, we reply.

Lena says she and Vilmos have to go to Zagreb for two nights. She doesn't say why. She says we can stay, but the moment their car disappears on Glavna ulica in the far distance, the magic of Kneževi Vinogradi is gone. We pack our stuff, put the key under the foot mat in front of the door, get into the rental car, and drive to the coast. The old woman in Vodice who rents the room on the second floor above her living room doesn't speak English, nor German. She has a big wart on her back. We keep staring at it as we follow her up the staircase, whose terracotta floors look institutional. The room in Vodice is a plain cell. There is a bed and a reproduction of a painting of a saint with a golden halo above it. The saint looks friendly. We tell him that we have been married for eighteen years before we go to bed. There is a small balcony and when we step out, far in the distance, we can see the Adriatic Sea. We go there. The beach is covered with half-naked bodies. They are lying around everywhere, even on the promenade. There is no shade at the beach. Many of the bodies are badly sunburned. It feels like the Middle Ages.

We find a girl who rents us her father's motorboat. The next morning, we go out into the sea. The sea is blue and big. The boat is small. We have a map, and on that map, we circled a small island. Small islands, we wrote in our unsuccessful ap-

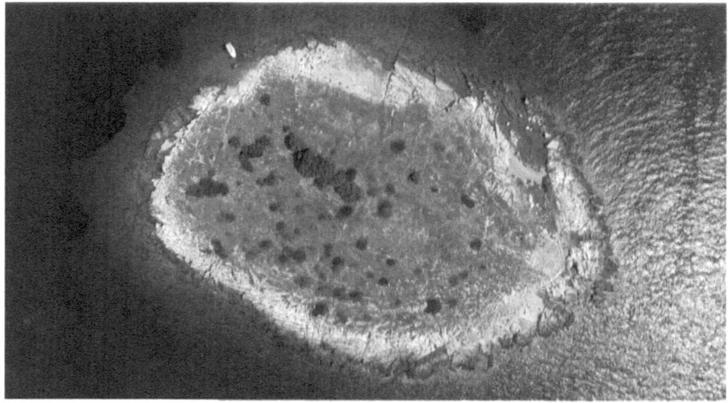

plication to the Ministry of Culture of Croatia, are places that (dis)appear due to high tides of the sea. We want to be on these islands and learn what it means to be an island in the sea, we wrote. Who knows, we wrote. It might be the perseverance of very small islands that constantly get washed over by the ocean, which could provide assistance in reshaping the ways in which we picture *invisibility*. A small island might offer clues of how it was possible that on March 8, 2014, while flying from Kuala Lumpur International Airport, Malaysia, to Beijing Capital

International Airport in China, the Malaysian Airliner MH370 with 239 people onboard *disappeared*, despite the omnipresence of surveillance technologies supposedly covering the globe.

Since we have no cell phone reception on the sea, we locate the island with our eyes. We drive around it with the boat two times. The island is round. We throw the anchor into the water on the side where the shore is shallow and step on the island. It's a strange step. It takes twenty minutes to walk around the island's outer perimeters. We think of the Czech man. How he brought a flag and a pole, how limiting that feels to us. We walk toward the center of the island, which is probably ten meters above sea level. There are six pine trees there. They provide shade. Thank you pine trees, we say. We walk back to the boat, unload our equipment, put everything under the trees, and sit down. This is our base, we say, as a cicada starts hum-whistling right above our heads. We look for this loud creature screaming its mating call out into the world without any sense of modesty—intensely shrill and repetitive. We look and look, but we can't find him. We scan the branches of one of the trees. He keeps buzzing. We keep scanning. Suddenly he stops. We sit down on the ground, which is covered with brown needles, and look at the Adriatic Sea. It's blue; not just one blue, but many different blues—greenish blue, navy blue, admiral blue, azure, cobalt, denim, ultramarine, Persian blue. There are sailboats out there. The cicada starts again. We go back to scan-

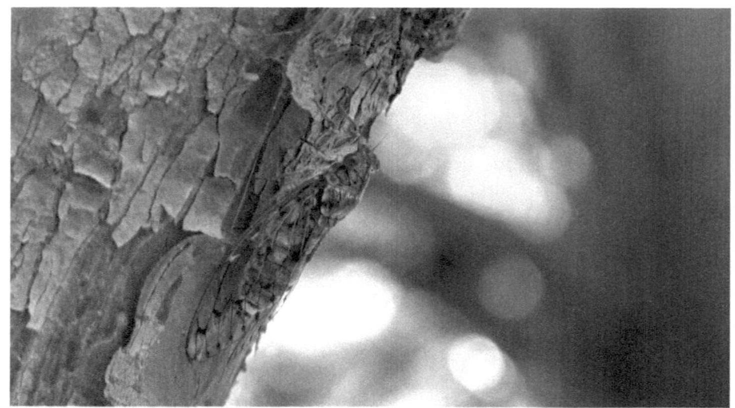

ning the tree. We do it more systematically this time, first the trunk, up and down, then every branch, every needle, until finally we find him. His body looks like the bark of the branch. Even when we look at him, it takes some effort to remind ourselves that we are actually *seeing him*, and when he starts buzzing again, it's even harder to believe that this shrill sound comes from something so hard to discern. We get the drone out and let it circumference the island. We hide under the trees while it circles the island three times. On the screen it looks as if the island is devoid of humans. Our abandoned white boat looks tiny. The scene on the screen looks either like the beginning or the end of a movie. It's hard to tell. We go to the shore and wade around. There is trash in the water. Pieces of tiles, pieces of glass, old batteries, metal parts, plastic—we start sifting through it. This is the cleanest trash there is, we say. It has been washed and sterilized by the salt water for many years. We name some pieces and speculate where they are coming from. We start thinking of categories. Glass, metal, plastic, fiber, tiles, mixed materials. The more we look, the more trash we find. At one point, it dawns on us that the whole island is actually covered with trash. We've landed on an overgrown dumpster, we say. No wonder nobody else is here. We get a plastic bag and start collecting. We lay out what we collected on large, flat rocks and start photographing the displays. We keep looking and collecting and photographing, until suddenly we feel very sick. We've been in the sun for too long without drinking any water; we've been going through the trash without taking a break. The sun and the trash have taken their toll. We need to lay down. The water is very salty. If one spreads out evenly, one automatically floats. We lay down on the surface of the water. We close our eyes and start floating. We feel the waves as

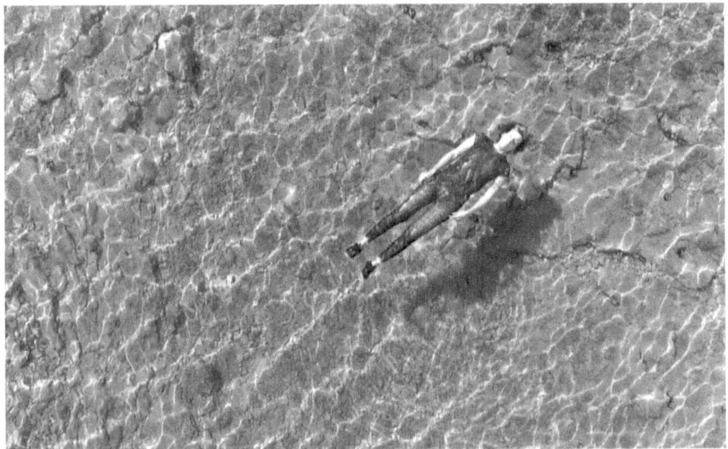

they are crashing against the shore, feel how they bounce back more gently. We imagine the drone being right above us. Right above our bodies, very close. We can feel the wind its propellers are making on our arms and legs and on our chest and on our faces; we feel the ripples in the water the wind is making around the outlines of our bodies. Then the wind gets less and less noticeable. The drone is rising, we imagine, it gets further and further away, flies higher and higher up into the sky, and we get smaller and smaller and smaller and smaller and smaller and smaller

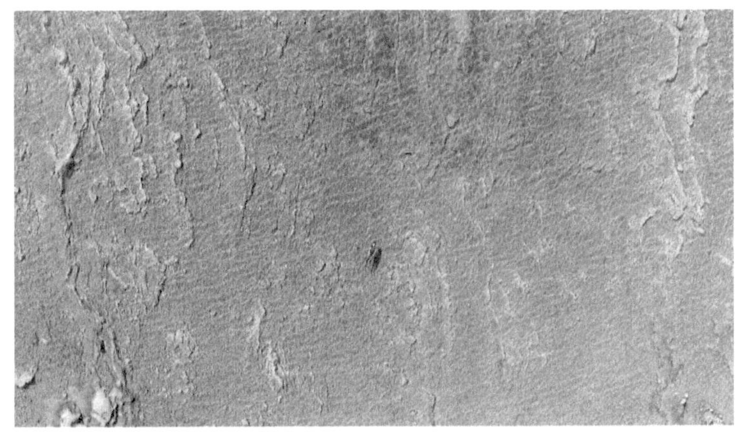

There are many people we have to thank for helping us to
realize this project, but the most important ones were
Zeljka Himbele, Lea Vene, Ana Kovačić and
Isolde Moderegger.
Hvala
and
thank you
Hillit Zwick and Melissa Ragona for feedback on the writing.
Copy Editing: Brianna Goodman

The project was financially supported through a grant from the
City of Zagreb City Office for Education, Culture and Sports
The exhibition was supported by FACE Croatia and a travel
grant from The City College.

all images by eteam,
except images on page 43 "Bosnian Girl", 2003 by Šejla Kamerić,
on page 44 and 78 are images from wikipedia, on page 94 is a screenshot
from google earth and on page 106 is a screenshot from a youtube video of
a Liberland conference.

Books we read around the time of our research trip:

The Origins of Totalitarianism by Hannah Arendt
The Emigrants by W.G. Sebald
The Warren Commission Report at the National Archives online
The Art of War by Sun Tzu
The Sunflower: On the Possibilities and Limits of Forgiveness by Simon Wiesenthal

We did not read "*Van Goghs Ohr: Paul Gauguin und der Pakt des Schweigens* (Van Gogh's Ear: Paul Gauguin and the Pact of Silence, Osburg) by Hans Kaufmann and Rita Wildegans, only read a short article about them arguing that Vincent van Gogh may have made up the whole story about cutting off his own ear in order to protect Gauguin.

www.ingramcontent.com/pod-product-compliance
Lightning Source LLC
Chambersburg PA
CBHW031344060726
47590CB00007B/2612